Southern Living

Salads
Cookbook
By Jean Wickstrom
Assistant Foods Editor

Copyright© 1975 by Oxmoor House, Inc.
Book Division of Southern Progress Corporation
P.O. Box 2463, Birmingham, Alabama 35201

Library of Congress Catalog Card Number: 74-18644
ISBN: 0-8487-0367-7

Manufactured in the United States of America

Fourth Printing 1982

Illustrations: Carol Middleton
Cover: Taylor Lewis

You might imagine there is more to salad making than tossing a few greens and tomatoes in the familiar wooden bowl. But too often, as cooks, our creativity is channeled into the "main dish" rather than into the salad. *Salads Cookbook* is designed to change your thinking and to provide you with hundreds of salad choices so that a salad might well be your main dish.

Introduction

There is no denying that salads add interest and zest to a meal; they are not only good, they are good for you. Fruits and vegetables are two of the chief sources of vitamins A and C. And, happily, fruits and vegetables, along with greens, are the primary ingredients in salads, particularly accompaniment salads, which remain the perennial favorites. Meat, seafood, cheese, and eggs are prime choices for hearty and nutritious main-dish salads, meals in themselves. This cookbook devotes a chapter to each of these ingredients to provide you with an array of recipes that will surely add color, flavor, and texture to your meals. Additionally, there are chapters on delicious salad variations: molded fruit and molded vegetable salads; and frozen salads, many of which are equally delightful as desserts.

Be it an accompaniment or main dish, a salad needs a setting of crisp greens and a zesty dressing to enhance its flavor. The cookbook includes tips on the varieties of greens and their care, as well as a careful selection of dressing recipes to add that finishing touch. And for those of you who have often admired a beautiful salad tray garnished with radish roses, mushroom whirls, and onion chrysanthemums, *Salads Cookbook* will show you how it is done.

4

Fruit Salad

SPICED PEACH SALAD

    1 teaspoon ground cinnamon
1/2 teaspoon ground cloves
    1 teaspoon ground allspice
3/4 cup firmly packed brown sugar
1/2 cup cider vinegar
    1 (29-ounce) can peach halves, drained,
        liquid reserved
3/4 cup peach liquid
    1 (3-ounce) package cream cheese,
        softened
        Half-and-half

Mix spices, brown sugar, and vinegar with peach liquid. Bring to a boil, reduce heat and simmer for 5 minutes. Pour mixture over peach halves while hot. Let sit for several hours or overnight. Before serving, combine cream cheese and enough half-and-half to make smooth mixture. Place a teaspoon of this mixture in center of each peach half. Yield: 7 to 8 servings.

CITRUS SALAD

    Crisp salad greens
    Orange sections
    Grapefruit sections
    Maraschino cherries (optional)
    Orange French Dressing

Line salad bowl or individual plates with salad greens. Arrange orange and grapefruit sections on greens. Garnish with cherries, if desired. Serve Orange French Dressing with salad.

Orange French Dressing:

    1 (6-ounce) can frozen orange juice
        concentrate, undiluted
3/4 cup salad oil
1/4 cup vinegar
    3 tablespoons sugar
1/2 teaspoon dry mustard
1/4 teaspoon salt
1/4 teaspoon hot sauce

Combine all ingredients. Chill. Yield: 1 3/4 cups dressing.

APPLE-WALNUT SALAD

2/3 cup mayonnaise
    1 tablespoon lemon juice
    1 tablespoon sugar
1/8 teaspoon salt
    3 red apples
    1 cup diced celery
1/3 cup chopped walnuts
        Salad greens
        Sliced oranges, grapes

Combine mayonnaise, lemon juice, sugar, and salt. Peel and dice apples (leave skin on half an apple to add color to salad). Stir into mayonnaise mixture. Add celery and walnuts. Serve on salad greens, and garnish with oranges and grapes. Yield: 6 servings.

DELLA ROBBIA SALAD

1 head lettuce
1 (16-ounce) can peach halves, chilled and drained
2 (16-ounce) cans pear halves, chilled and drained
1 (20-ounce) can pineapple slices, chilled and drained
1 (17-ounce) can peeled whole apricots, chilled and drained
1 (16-ounce) jar crabapples, chilled and drained
 Seedless grapes, chilled
 Parsley or mint
 Favorite fruit dressing

Arrange bed of crisp lettuce on large round platter. Around outer rim place peach and pear halves in pairs to resemble whole fruit. Cut pineapple slices in half, placing 2 half-slices between each peach and pear. Arrange apricots and crabapples alternately in inner circle. Place grapes in center and garnish with parsley or mint.

Serve with fruit dressing. Yield: 10 to 12 servings.

CHERRY-PECAN WALDORF SALAD

1 cup chopped unpeeled apples
2 tablespoons chopped maraschino cherries
1/2 cup chopped pecans
1/2 cup diced celery
1/2 cup mayonnaise or salad dressing
 Lettuce leaves

Combine fruit, pecans, celery, and mayonnaise or salad dressing. Chill and serve on crisp lettuce leaves. Yield: 4 servings.

ISLAND FRUIT SALAD

1 small fresh pineapple, cut into chunks
1 small cantaloupe, cut into balls
1 fresh pear, sliced
2 bananas, sliced
1 cup sliced strawberries
2 oranges, sectioned, cut into bite-size pieces
1 cup seedless grapes
 Lemon juice
 Fruit Dressing

Dip all fruits in lemon juice; combine fruits and chill in covered container. Pour Fruit Dressing over fruit, blend well, and serve cold. Yield: 4 generous servings.

Fruit Dressing:

1/2 to 3/4 cup orange juice
1/4 cup salad oil
 1 tablespoon sugar
1/2 teaspoon salt
1/2 teaspoon paprika
1/4 teaspoon celery seeds
1/2 clove garlic, crushed

Combine all ingredients in jar; shake gently to blend. Cover and chill several hours before serving on fruit salad. Yield: 1 1/4 cups.

SUNNY SALAD

1 medium-size avocado, peeled
 Lemon juice
1 (16-ounce) can pear halves, drained
 Lettuce
 Mayonnaise (optional)

Slice avocado into thin wedges; dip into lemon juice. Arrange pears and avocado on lettuce-lined plates. Top with mayonnaise, if desired. Yield: 4 to 6 servings.

RAW CRANBERRY SALAD

2 cups (1/2 pound) fresh cranberries
1 cup sugar
1 cup diced unpeeled apples
1 cup grape halves
1 cup orange sections
1/2 cup chopped pecans or walnuts
    Lettuce
4 tablespoons whipping cream, whipped
1/4 cup mayonnaise

Wash cranberries and put through a food chopper, using coarse blade. Add sugar, and let drain overnight in refrigerator. (Save juice to use in punch or molded salads.) Combine cranberries, apples, grapes, oranges, and nuts. Toss lightly. Serve on lettuce. Blend whipped cream with mayonnaise and serve over salad. Yield: 8 servings.

GRAPE AND CABBAGE SALAD

1 cup green seedless grapes
1 cup seeded grapes
3 cups shredded cabbage
1 1/2 teaspoons salt
1/8 teaspoon freshly ground black pepper
1 tablespoon lemon juice
1/4 cup mayonnaise
    Head lettuce
    Whole fresh grapes for garnish (optional)

Combine grapes, cabbage, salt, pepper, lemon juice, and mayonnaise; toss lightly. Serve on lettuce leaves. Garnish with additional grapes, if desired. Yield: 6 servings.

DATE SALAD

2 (3-ounce) packages cream cheese, softened
1/2 pint whipping cream, whipped
1 (8-ounce) package dates, chopped
1 (8 1/4-ounce) can crushed pineapple, drained
1 cup chopped pecans
1/2 teaspoon vanilla extract

Combine cream cheese and whipped cream. Add dates, pineapple, pecans, and vanilla. Mix and chill at least 1 hour before serving. Yield: 6 to 8 servings.

CELERY AND APPLE SALAD

2 eggs, separated
1/2 cup milk
1/2 cup sugar
2 tablespoons cornstarch
    Juice of 3 lemons
    Pinch salt
2 cups chopped apples
3/4 to 1 cup chopped celery
3/4 cup white seedless raisins

Beat egg whites; add yolks and beat again. Add milk and mix well. Combine sugar and cornstarch in top of double boiler; add egg-milk mixture and stir well. Add lemon juice and salt and cook until thickened. Allow to cool.

Combine apples, celery, and raisins. Add cooled dressing and mix well. Yield: 6 servings.

PEACH-COTTAGE CHEESE SALAD

- 2/3 cup orange juice
-   2 tablespoons all-purpose flour
-   2 tablespoons sugar
    Pinch salt
- 1/4 teaspoon dry mustard
- 1/2 teaspoon grated orange rind
-   1 to 2 teaspoons vinegar
-   4 tablespoons mayonnaise
-   2 tablespoons milk
-   1 (29-ounce) can peach halves, drained
    Lettuce
-   1 cup cottage cheese
- 1/4 cup sliced dates
- 1/4 cup slivered toasted almonds
-   1 tablespoon grated orange rind

Heat orange juice. Combine flour, sugar, salt, and mustard; stir to blend. Add to hot juice, and cook and stir until mixture thickens. Remove from heat and blend in the 1/2 teaspoon orange rind and vinegar. Cool; stir in mayonnaise and milk.

Place each peach half on lettuce leaf. Combine cottage cheese, dates, almonds, and the 1 tablespoon orange rind. Mound this mixture on peach halves, and top with sauce. Yield: 8 servings.

FRUIT PLATE WITH ORANGE MAYONNAISE

    Fresh fruit
    Lemon or orange juice
-   1 cup mayonnaise
- 1/4 cup orange juice
    Dash ground allspice

Cut fresh fruit into bite-size pieces or quarters; brush lemon or orange juice over cut surfaces of fruit that would turn dark. Arrange fruit on platter.

Combine mayonnaise, 1/4 cup orange juice, and allspice for a fruit dressing. Chill. Spoon over fruit. Yield: 1 1/2 cups.

HARVEST BOWL SALAD

-   2 eggs
- 1/4 cup sugar
    Dash salt
-   2 tablespoons lemon juice
- 2/3 cup whipping cream, whipped
-   2 cups chopped apples
-   1 (8-ounce) can pineapple chunks, drained
-   1 cup grapes, cut in halves
-   2 bananas, sliced
- 1/2 cup chopped pecans
- 1/2 cup diced celery

Beat eggs slightly; add sugar, salt, and lemon juice and cook in top of double boiler until thick, stirring constantly. Cool. Fold whipped cream into cooled egg mixture. Combine fruit, pecans, and celery and fold in dressing mixture. Yield: 6 servings.

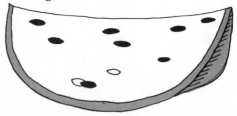

TWENTY-FOUR-HOUR SOUR CREAM SALAD

-   1 (17-ounce) can spiced grapes, drained
-   1 (11-ounce) can mandarin oranges, drained
-   1 (13 1/4-ounce) can pineapple chunks, drained
-   6 or 8 maraschino cherries, sliced
-   2 cups miniature marshmallows
-   1 cup commercial sour cream

Combine fruit and marshmallows; let sit 1 hour. Fold in sour cream. Place in covered bowl or casserole. Chill 24 hours before serving. Fruit cocktail may be substituted for grapes and oranges. Yield: 8 to 10 servings.

EDEN SALAD

1 cup dried figs
1 cup diced apples
1/2 cup diced celery
   Commercial French dressing
   Lettuce
   Mayonnaise

Boil figs 5 minutes in enough water to cover; drain and cut into strips. Combine figs, apples, and celery. Add enough French dressing to moisten. Serve on lettuce; top with mayonnaise. Yield: 4 servings.

TROPICAL STUFFED AVOCADO SALAD

2 tablespoons lemon juice
2 tablespoons honey
1 cup orange sections, halved
1 cup grapefruit sections, halved
1 cup pineapple wedges
3 avocados
   Lemon juice

Combine 2 tablespoons lemon juice and honey; marinate oranges, grapefruit, and pineapple 1 hour in this mixture. Cut avocados in half lengthwise and remove pits. Brush inside of avocados with lemon juice. Fill cavities with fruit mixture. Yield: 6 servings.

BANANA-PEANUT SALAD

1 teaspoon all-purpose flour
1 tablespoon sugar
1/2 teaspoon dry mustard
1 tablespoon butter
1 egg, well beaten
2 tablespoons vinegar
6 bananas, peeled and cut in half
   Crushed or ground peanuts
   Lettuce

Combine flour, sugar, and mustard; add butter, egg, and vinegar. Cook over medium heat until mixture thickens.

Slice bananas; roll in salad dressing, then in ground peanuts. Serve on lettuce leaves. Yield: 6 servings.

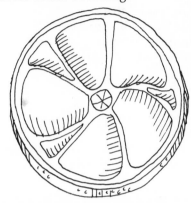

PEACH-OLIVE SALAD WITH LIME DRESSING

1 (12-ounce) carton cottage cheese
3/4 cup chopped ripe olives
1/4 teaspoon salt
   Salad greens
1 (29-ounce) can peach halves, drained
   Paprika
   Chopped nuts
   Lime Dressing

Combine cottage cheese, olives, and salt; mound on salad greens with peach halves arranged on side. Fill peach centers with additional cheese mixture. Sprinkle with paprika and nuts. Serve with Lime Dressing. Yield: 4 to 5 servings.

Lime Dressing:

1/2 cup salad oil
1/2 cup lime juice
1/2 teaspoon salt
2 tablespoons honey or sugar
   Dash cayenne pepper

Combine all ingredients and shake well. Yield: 1 cup.

9

GRAPE SALAD

1 (8-ounce) package cream cheese, softened
1 (15 1/4-ounce) can crushed pineapple, drained, liquid reserved
1/2 cup pineapple juice
4 cups seedless white grapes
2/3 cup chopped nuts
1 (6-ounce) package miniature marshmallows
Lettuce

Blend cream cheese and pineapple liquid until smooth. Add pineapple, grapes, nuts, and marshmallows. Mix well and chill several hours. Serve on lettuce leaves. Yield: 6 to 8 servings.

MAKE-AHEAD FRUIT SALAD

1/2 cup mayonnaise
1/4 pint whipping cream, whipped
1 tablespoon lemon juice
1 (29-ounce) can peach slices, drained
1 cup miniature marshmallows
1/2 cup maraschino cherries, halved
1 banana, sliced
1/4 cup chopped nuts

Combine mayonnaise, whipped cream, and lemon juice; mix until well blended. Fold in remaining ingredients; chill. This salad may be made hours ahead; it tastes even better when the fruit flavors mingle longer with the marshmallows and whipped cream. Yield: 8 servings.

COOKED APPLE SALAD

6 apples, unpeeled, cored
1/2 (8-ounce) package cream cheese, softened
Mayonnaise or cream
1/4 cup chopped nuts

In a covered pan, cook apples in a small amount of water until they are tender but not mushy. Remove from water and remove peel. Combine cream cheese, a small amount of mayonnaise or cream, and nuts; fill apples with this mixture. Chill and serve with additional mayonnaise. Yield: 6 servings.

APRICOT SALAD

1 (17-ounce) can apricots, drained, liquid reserved
1/4 pound Cheddar cheese, shredded
1 cup chopped pecans
1/2 cup sugar
2 tablespoons all-purpose flour
1 egg

In a flat dish place a layer of apricots, a layer of cheese, and a layer of pecans. Combine apricot liquid, sugar, flour, and egg in a saucepan; cook until thickened. Pour over fruit-cheese mixture and chill before serving. Yield: 8 servings.

GINGERED PEAR SALAD

8 to 10 gingersnaps, finely crushed
1 (3-ounce) package cream cheese, softened
1 tablespoon whipping cream
6 to 8 canned pear halves, chilled and drained
Crisp lettuce

Combine gingersnaps, cream cheese, and whipping cream and mix well. Place pear halves on lettuce; fill cavities with cream cheese mixture. Yield: 6 to 8 servings.

Molded Fruit Salads

Dissolve gelatin in hot water; allow to cool. Add lemon juice and salt; chill. Blend together mayonnaise, avocado puree, and whipped cream or evaporated milk. Fold into thickened gelatin mixture. Pour mixture into a mold and chill. Yield: 6 servings.

CHERRY SALAD

- 1 (17-ounce) can pitted dark sweet cherries, drained, liquid reserved
- 1/3 cup lemon juice
- 1 (3-ounce) package orange-flavored gelatin
- 1 (3-ounce) bottle stuffed olives, sliced
- 3/4 cup chopped pecans

Combine cherry liquid, lemon juice, and enough water to make 1 3/4 cups. Heat liquid to boiling, pour over gelatin, and stir until dissolved. Chill until partially set. Add cherries, olives, and pecans. Pour into a 1-quart mold and chill until firm. Yield: 8 servings.

AVOCADO SALAD

- 1 cup boiling water
- 1 (3-ounce) package lemon-flavored gelatin
- 1 cup commercial sour cream
- 3/4 to 1 cup mayonnaise
- 1 cup (1 large) mashed avocado
- 3 tablespoons lemon juice (optional)
  Mint leaves or parsley

Pour boiling water over gelatin and stir until dissolved. Cool. Add sour cream, mayonnaise, avocado, and lemon juice, if desired. Mix well. Pour into ring mold or individual molds which have been rinsed in cold water. Chill until firm. Garnish with mint leaves or parsley. Yield: 6 to 8 servings.

AVOCADO-GELATIN SALAD

- 1 (3-ounce) package lemon-flavored gelatin
- 3/4 cup hot water
- 2 tablespoons lemon juice
- 1 teaspoon salt
- 1/2 cup mayonnaise
- 1 cup frozen avocado puree, slightly thawed
- 1/4 pint whipping cream or 1/2 cup evaporated milk, whipped

FROSTED CHERRY SALAD

1 (17-ounce) can red sour cherries, undrained
1/2 cup sugar
1 (3-ounce) package cherry-flavored gelatin
3/4 cup cold water
2/3 cup finely chopped celery
1 (3-ounce) package cream cheese, softened
2 tablespoons mayonnaise
1/4 cup chopped pecans

Combine cherries, sugar, and gelatin in a saucepan; heat until gelatin is dissolved. Add cold water and cool. Chill until it begins to thicken. Add celery and return to refrigerator. When congealed, top with mixture of softened cream cheese and mayonnaise. Sprinkle with pecans. Chill until serving time. Yield: 4 servings.

APRICOT-CHEESE SALAD

2 (3-ounce) packages orange-flavored gelatin
2 cups boiling water
1 (17-ounce) can apricots, drained, liquid reserved
1 (20-ounce) can crushed pineapple, drained, liquid reserved
2 cups combined apricot and pineapple liquid, divided
1 cup miniature marshmallows
Topping

Dissolve gelatin in boiling water. Cut each apricot into 3 pieces. Combine fruits and marshmallows. Add 1 cup of combined liquid to gelatin and reserve remaining liquid. Chill until thickened and fold in fruits and marshmallows. Pour into a lightly oiled 12- x 8-inch pan and spread with Topping.

Topping:

1 envelope (1 tablespoon) unflavored gelatin
1/4 cup cold water
1/2 cup sugar
3 tablespoons all-purpose flour
1 egg, slightly beaten
1 cup combined apricot and pineapple liquid
2 tablespoons butter
Juice and grated rind of 1 lemon
1/2 pint whipping cream, whipped
1 cup shredded cheese
Lettuce

Dissolve gelatin in cold water. Combine sugar, flour, egg, and fruit liquid in double boiler. Stir in gelatin, butter, lemon juice, and rind. Continue cooking and stirring to blend. When cool fold in whipped cream and spread over salad. Sprinkle top with cheese and serve in squares on lettuce. Salad is best if made the day before serving. Yield: 12 servings.

AVOCADO-PINEAPPLE SALAD

1 (3-ounce) package lime-flavored gelatin
1 (8 1/4-ounce) can crushed pineapple, drained, liquid reserved
3/4 cup mayonnaise
1/2 pint whipping cream, whipped
1 avocado, mashed
Chopped nuts (optional)

Prepare gelatin according to package directions, using juice drained from pineapple as part of the liquid. Chill until mixture is texture of unbeaten egg white. Fold in pineapple, mayonnaise, whipped cream, avocado, and nuts, if desired. Put into a 1-quart mold and chill until firm. Yield: 8 to 10 servings.

CHERRY JUBILEE SALAD

1 (17-ounce) can pitted dark sweet
    cherries, drained, liquid reserved
1/2 cup currant jelly
1/2 cup sherry
1 (3-ounce) package black cherry-
    flavored gelatin
4 tablespoons lemon juice
1/2 cup chopped pecans

Combine cherry liquid, jelly, and
sherry in saucepan; bring to a boil and stir
until jelly has melted. Pour over gelatin
and stir until gelatin has dissolved. Cool
slightly and add lemon juice and cherries.
Chill until partially set; stir in pecans.
Chill until firm. Yield: 6 servings.

MOLDED SWEET CHERRY SALAD

1 (17-ounce) can light sweet cherries,
    drained and pitted, liquid reserved
    Boiling water
1 (3-ounce) package cherry-flavored
    gelatin
8 stuffed olives, chopped
1 cup slivered almonds, toasted and
    chopped
    Crisp lettuce
    Mayonnaise

Measure separately the reserved cherry
liquid and enough boiling water to make
2 cups, but do not combine. Dissolve
gelatin in boiling water; then add cherry
liquid. Chill until thick and syrupy. Fold
cherries, olives, and almonds into slightly
thickened gelatin. Pour into a 5-cup mold
and chill until firm. Unmold on crisp
lettuce and garnish with mayonnaise.
Yield: 6 servings.

CONGEALED AVOCADO SALAD

1 (3-ounce) package lime-flavored
    gelatin
1 cup boiling water
1 (3-ounce) package cream cheese,
    softened
1 avocado, chopped
1 small onion, finely chopped
2 stalks celery, chopped
1 pimiento, chopped
1/2 cup mayonnaise

Dissolve gelatin in boiling water. Chill
until syrupy. Combine cream cheese with
other ingredients and add to gelatin
mixture. Spoon into 8 individual molds,
and chill until set. Yield: 8 servings.

GRAPEFRUIT-LIME RING MOLD

1 (3-ounce) package cream cheese,
    softened
1 cup boiling water
2 (3-ounce) packages lime-flavored
    gelatin
1 quart grapefruit sections, drained,
    liquid reserved
2 cups grapefruit liquid
    Maraschino cherries
    Salad greens

Shape cheese into 8 balls; chill. Add
boiling water to gelatin in saucepan and
stir over low heat until completely
dissolved. Add grapefruit liquid. Spoon
gelatin mixture into a 5-cup ring mold to
cover bottom; over this arrange 8
grapefruit sections, cherries, and cheese
balls. Slowly spoon in gelatin mixture to
barely cover fruit; chill until almost firm.
Chill remaining gelatin mixture until
syrupy; fold in remaining grapefruit.
Spoon over first layer. Chill until firm. To
serve, unmold on salad greens and fill
center with additional fruit as desired.
Yield: 8 servings.

MOLDED COTTAGE CHEESE AND GRAPE SALAD

2 cups cottage cheese
1/2 teaspoon salt
1/8 teaspoon white pepper
1 cup milk
1/3 cup mayonnaise
2 envelopes (2 tablespoons) unflavored gelatin
1/2 cup cold water
2 cups green seedless grapes, divided
1 cup seeded grapes
Commercial salad dressing

Put cottage cheese through a sieve and mix with the next 4 ingredients. Soften gelatin in cold water and dissolve over hot water. Stir into cottage cheese mixture. Chill until thickened. Fold in 1 cup of green grapes. Turn into a greased ring mold. Chill until firm. Turn onto a serving plate. Fill center with remaining grapes mixed together. Serve with your favorite salad dressing. Yield: 8 servings.

BLUEBERRY SALAD

2 (3-ounce) packages blackberry-flavored gelatin
2 cups boiling water
1 (15-ounce) can blueberries, drained, liquid reserved
1 (8 1/4-ounce) can crushed pineapple, drained, liquid reserved
1 (8-ounce) package cream cheese, softened
1/2 cup sugar
1 cup commercial sour cream
1/2 teaspoon vanilla extract
1/2 cup chopped pecans

Dissolve gelatin in boiling water. Add liquid drained from fruit and enough water to make 1 cup. Stir in blueberries and pineapple. Pour into a 2-quart flat pan, cover, and chill until firm.
Combine cream cheese, sugar, sour cream, and vanilla; spread over congealed salad. Sprinkle with chopped pecans. Yield: 10 to 12 servings.

LEMONADE SALAD

1 (17-ounce) can fruit cocktail, drained, liquid reserved
1 (6-ounce) package lemon-flavored gelatin
1 (12-ounce) can frozen lemonade concentrate, undiluted
1/2 cup chopped nuts

Heat fruit liquid to boiling. Add gelatin and stir until dissolved; add lemonade. Chill until partially set. Stir in fruit cocktail and nuts. Spoon into a 1-quart mold and chill until firm. Yield: 6 servings.

ORANGE-WATER CHESTNUT SALAD

1 (11-ounce) can mandarin oranges, drained, liquid reserved
1 (3-ounce) package orange-flavored gelatin
1 (6-ounce) can water chestnuts, sliced paper-thin
Mayonnaise

Measure mandarin liquid and add enough hot water to make 1 1/2 cups. Heat to boiling; add gelatin and stir until gelatin dissolves. Chill until gelatin begins to thicken. Add orange sections and water chestnuts. Spoon into a 6-cup mold and chill until firm. Serve with mayonnaise. Yield: 6 servings.

GRAPEFRUIT RING MOLD

1 (16-ounce) can grapefruit sections,
   drained, liquid reserved
1 (18-ounce) can grapefruit juice
2 envelopes (2 tablespoons) unflavored
   gelatin
8 stuffed olives, sliced
   Salad greens

Add drained liquid to grapefruit juice;
measure. Add enough water to make 3 1/2
cups. Soften gelatin in 1 cup of the liquid.
Heat remaining liquid and add softened
gelatin; stir until dissolved. Chill until
consistency of unbeaten egg white.

Arrange some of the grapefruit sections
and sliced olives in bottom of a 5-cup ring
mold. Add enough of the chilled mixture
to cover sections and olive slices. Chill
until almost firm.

Repeat procedure, reserving some of
the grapefruit sections and olive slices.
Chill until firm. Unmold on serving
platter. Surround grapefruit ring with
salad greens and garnish with remaining
grapefruit sections and olive slices. If
desired, fill center with salad greens,
chicken salad, tuna fish salad, or cottage
cheese. Yield: 8 servings.

JELLIED GRAPE SALAD

2 envelopes (2 tablespoons) unflavored
   gelatin
1/2 cup cold water
1 cup hot water
1/2 cup sugar
1/4 teaspoon salt
1 cup orange juice
1/2 cup lemon juice
1 cup green seedless grapes
1 cup seeded Malaga grapes
1 cup seeded Ribier grapes
   Head lettuce
   Mayonnaise

Soften gelatin in cold water. Add hot
water, sugar, and salt; stir until dissolved.
Add orange and lemon juice. Chill until
about the consistency of unbeaten egg
white. Fold in grapes. Spoon into a 5-cup
mold. Chill until firm. Turn onto a serving
plate. Serve with lettuce and mayonnaise.
Yield: 8 servings.

BLUEBERRY CONGEALED SALAD

1 (6-ounce) package raspberry-flavored
   gelatin
1 cup boiling water
1 envelope (1 tablespoon) unflavored
   gelatin
1/4 cup old water
1 (20-ounce) can crushed pineapple,
   drained, liquid reserved and chilled
1 (15-ounce) can blueberries, drained,
   liquid reserved and chilled
   Orange juice
1 cup cold water
1/2 pint whipping cream
2 tablespoons sugar
1 cup chopped pecans

Dissolve raspberry gelatin in boiling
water. Add unflavored gelatin to 1/4 cup
cold water and stir until softened. Add to
raspberry gelatin and stir until dissolved.
Measure liquid from fruits; add orange
juice, if needed, to make 1 1/2 cups. Add
to gelatin mixture. Stir in cold water. Chill
until mixture begins to congeal.

Combine cream,—which has been
whipped with 2 tablespoons sugar
—fruits, and pecans. Add to gelatin
mixture; spoon into a 5-cup mold and
chill until firm. Yield: 6 to 8 servings.

15

CRANBERRY SALAD

1 (8 1/4-ounce) can crushed pineapple, drained, liquid reserved
1 envelope (1 tablespoon) unflavored gelatin
3/4 cup cranberry sauce
2 cups water
1 (3-ounce) package cherry-flavored gelatin
1/2 cup chopped celery
1/2 cup chopped pecans

Add enough water to pineapple liquid to make 1/2 cup. Soak unflavored gelatin in this mixture. Dissolve cranberry sauce over low heat. When dissolved add water and heat well. Dissolve cherry gelatin and unflavored gelatin mixture in hot cranberry mixture. Add pineapple, celery, and pecans. Pour into a mold and chill until congealed. Yield: 8 to 10 servings.

CRANBERRY DELIGHT SALAD

1 (16-ounce) can cranberry sauce
1 cup commercial sour cream
 Dash salt
1 cup diced marshmallows
1 envelope (1 tablespoon) unflavored gelatin
3/4 cup canned plums, drained, pitted, diced, and liquid reserved
1/2 cup plum liquid
1/2 cup diced celery
1/2 cup chopped walnuts

Beat cranberry sauce, sour cream, and salt with rotary beater; add marshmallows. Soften gelatin in liquid from plums; dissolve this over hot water and add to cranberry mixture. Chill until partially thickened. Fold in plums, celery, and walnuts. Pour into individual molds and chill until firm. Yield: 6 servings.

GRAPE-WINE SALAD

2 envelopes (2 tablespoons) unflavored gelatin
1/2 cup cold water
3/4 cup boiling water
1/4 cup lemon juice
1 cup sugar
2 cups dry white wine
6 peach halves
1/4 pound white seedless grapes

Soften gelatin in cold water and dissolve in boiling water. Add lemon juice, sugar, and wine. Spoon a layer of gelatin into the bottom of a chilled 9-inch mold. Press peach halves around bottom and place a small cluster of grapes in center. Chill until almost set. Combine remaining grapes with gelatin and spoon over peach halves. Chill until firm. Unmold. Yield: 6 to 8 servings.

JELLIED CRANBERRY RELISH

2 oranges, quartered and seeded
1 quart cranberries
1 1/2 cups sugar
2 envelopes (2 tablespoons) unflavored gelatin
1 1/2 cups bottled cranberry juice cocktail

Put orange quarters and cranberries through food chopper using medium blade. Add sugar; mix well. In saucepan sprinkle gelatin on the cranberry juice cocktail to soften. Place over low heat, stirring constantly, until gelatin is dissolved. Remove from heat; stir into orange-cranberry relish. Turn into a 6-cup mold; chill until firm. Yield: 12 servings.

FRESH BLUEBERRY SALAD

2 (3-ounce) packages black cherry-
  flavored gelatin
3 cups boiling water
1 (8 1/4-ounce) can crushed pineapple,
  undrained
1/4 cup maraschino cherries, halved
2 cups fresh blueberries
  Salad Dressing

Dissolve gelatin in boiling water. Cool.
Add pineapple and chill until thickened.
Fold in cherries and blueberries. Chill
until firm. Serve with Salad Dressing.
Yield: 6 to 8 servings.

Salad Dressing:

1 cup miniature marshmallows
2 cups commercial sour cream
1 teaspoon mayonnaise
1/2 teaspoon vanilla extract

Combine all ingredients. Let stand
several hours or overnight in refrigerator.
Mix well and serve on Fresh Blueberry
Salad. Yield: 3 cups.

FRESH ORANGE-CRANBERRY JUICE SALAD

1 cup cranberry juice cocktail
1 (3-ounce) package lemon- or
  raspberry-flavored gelatin
2 oranges (about 1 cup), peeled and cut
  into bite-size pieces
1 cup commercial sour cream
1/4 cup chopped nuts

Heat cranberry juice cocktail to boiling;
remove from heat and stir in gelatin. Chill
until the consistency of unbeaten egg
white. Fold in orange pieces, sour cream,
and nuts. Chill until firm. Yield: 4 to 6
servings.

RIBBON SALAD

2 (3-ounce) packages lime-flavored
  gelatin
2 cups boiling water
1 1/2 cups cold water
2 (3-ounce) packages lemon-flavored
  gelatin
1 cup boiling water
1 (8-ounce) package cream cheese,
  softened
2 cups miniature marshmallows
1 (20-ounce) can crushed pineapple,
  drained, liquid reserved
1/2 pint whipping cream, whipped
2 (3-ounce) packages raspberry-
  flavored gelatin
2 cups boiling water
1 1/2 cups cold water

Dissolve lime gelatin in 2 cups boiling
water; add 1 1/2 cups cold water. Pour
into a 14- x 10- x 2-inch pan. Chill until
set.
Dissolve lemon gelatin in 1 cup boiling
water in top of double boiler. Add cream
cheese, which has been cut into small
pieces, and marshmallows; beat until well
blended. Remove from heat and stir in
pineapple and pineapple liquid. Cool;
fold in whipped cream. Spoon over top of
chilled lime gelatin. Chill until lemon
layer is firm.
Dissolve raspberry gelatin in 2 cups
boiling water. Add 1 1/2 cups cold water.
Cool; then pour over chilled lemon layer.
Chill until firm. Yield: 12 to 15 servings.

TWENTY-FOUR-HOUR SALAD

    2 eggs, beaten
1/4 cup vinegar
1/4 cup sugar
    2 tablespoons butter or margarine
    1 pint whipping cream, whipped
    2 cups light sweet cherries, drained,
        pitted, and halved
    2 cups pineapple chunks, drained
    2 cups orange slices, drained
    2 cups miniature marshmallows

Put eggs in top of a double boiler over low heat; add vinegar and sugar and beat constantly until mixture is thick and smooth. Remove from heat, add butter or margarine, and cool. When mixture is cold, fold in whipped cream, fruit, and marshmallows. Pour into a 2-quart mold and chill for 24 hours. Yield: 12 to 14 servings.

RASPBERRY SUPREME SALAD

    1 (3-ounce) package raspberry-flavored
        gelatin
    1 cup boiling water
    1 cup cold water
    2 medium-size bananas, diced
1/2 cup chopped nuts
2/3 cup flaked coconut
    1 (4-ounce) envelope whipped topping
        mix

Dissolve gelatin in boiling water; add cold water. Chill until mixture is consistency of honey. Add bananas, nuts, and coconut; mix well. Prepare whipped topping mix according to package directions and fold into gelatin mixture. Spoon into a 5-cup mold, or into individual molds, and chill until firm. Yield: 8 to 10 servings.

COUNTRY CLUB FRUIT SALAD

    1 (20-ounce) can pineapple chunks,
        drained, liquid reserved
    1 (17-ounce) can pitted dark sweet
        cherries, drained, liquid reserved
    1 (17-ounce) can or jar light sweet
        cherries, drained and pitted, liquid
        reserved
    1 cup sugar
    4 tablespoons cornstarch
1/4 teaspoon salt
3/4 cup orange juice
1/3 cup lemon juice
    3 egg yolks, slightly beaten
    2 envelopes (2 tablespoons) unflavored
        gelatin
1/4 cup cold water
    3 egg whites, stiffly beaten
    6 tablespoons sugar
1/2 pint whipping cream, whipped
    2 cups miniature marshmallows
    1 cup chopped pecans
    1 cup sliced strawberries
    2 (11-ounce) cans mandarin oranges,
        drained

Combine liquids from drained fruits, the 1 cup sugar, cornstarch, salt, orange juice, and lemon juice. Cook mixture over low heat, stirring constantly, until it begins to thicken. Stir a small amount of hot liquid into beaten egg yolks. Stir well; then add egg yolks to hot mixture. Continue cooking and stirring until mixture thickens.

Soften gelatin in cold water, add to cooked mixture, and stir until gelatin is dissolved. Remove from heat and chill about 30 minutes.

Into beaten egg whites stir the 6 tablespoons sugar and fold into chilled mixture. Chill. Fold in canned fruit, whipped cream, marshmallows, pecans, strawberries, and mandarin oranges. Chill until firm. Yield: 10 to 12 servings.

PLUM GELÉE

2 (30-ounce) cans plums, drained, liquid reserved
1 cup plum liquid
2 envelopes (2 tablespoons) unflavored gelatin
1/2 cup cold water
2 tablespoons lemon juice
1 cup seedless grapes
2 cups cantaloupe balls (or 1 cup cantaloupe and 1 cup honeydew melon)
Almond Mayonnaise

Pit plums and run through a food mill to make 3 cups puree (add some of the liquid to make 3 cups). Soften gelatin in cold water.

Heat plum puree with reserved plum liquid and dissolve gelatin in hot mixture. Add lemon juice and chill until syrupy. Fold in grapes and melon balls. Pour into a 7-cup mold and chill until firm. Serve with Almond Mayonnaise. Yield: 12 servings.

Almond Mayonnaise:

1 cup mayonnaise
1/4 cup slivered almonds
1/2 teaspoon almond extract

Combine all ingredients. Chill overnight. Yield: 1 1/4 cups.

STRAWBERRY DELIGHT SALAD

2 tablespoons sugar
2 cups sliced fresh strawberries
1 (3-ounce) package strawberry-flavored gelatin
1 cup boiling water
1/2 pound marshmallows
1/2 cup milk
1/2 pint whipping cream, whipped

Sprinkle sugar over berries; let stand 30 minutes. Dissolve gelatin in boiling water. Drain berries, reserving juice; add enough water to juice to make 1 cup and add to gelatin. Chill until partially set.

Combine marshmallows and milk. Heat in top of double boiler and stir until marshmallows melt; cool thoroughly, and fold in whipped cream. Add berries to gelatin and fold in marshmallow mixture. Pour into a 1-quart mold and chill until set. Yield: 6 servings.

ANGEL SALAD

2 (3-ounce) packages lime-flavored gelatin
2 cups hot water
1/3 envelope (1 teaspoon) unflavored gelatin
2 teaspoons cold water
2 (3-ounce) packages cream cheese, softened
1 (8 1/4-ounce) can crushed pineapple, drained
1 cup chopped celery
1 (2-ounce) jar pimientos, drained and chopped
1 cup chopped pecans
1/2 pint whipping cream, whipped

Dissolve lime gelatin in hot water. Soften unflavored gelatin in cold water; add to hot gelatin. Blend cheese and pineapple; add celery, pimientos, and pecans. Fold into cooled gelatin and chill until thick, but not firmly jelled. Fold in whipped cream. Pour into dampened mold and chill until firm. Yield: 12 servings.

PEACH PICKLE SALAD

8 pickled peaches, chopped, drained, liquid reserved
1 (3-ounce) package orange-flavored gelatin
1/3 cup chopped fresh parsley
1/2 cup chopped celery
1/2 cup chopped pecans

Combine peach liquid with enough water to make 2 cups; heat until boiling. Pour liquid over gelatin and stir until dissolved. Chill until slightly thickened. Add remaining ingredients. Pour into a 5-cup mold or individual molds. Chill until firm. Yield: 6 servings.

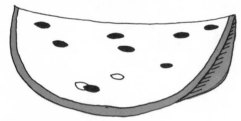

SPICED PEACH SALAD

1 cup diced canned peaches, drained, liquid reserved
3/4 cup peach liquid
1/4 cup vinegar
1/2 cup sugar
6 whole cloves
1 (1-inch) stick cinnamon
1 (3-ounce) package peach-flavored gelatin
1 cup boiling water

Combine peach liquid, vinegar, sugar, cloves, and cinnamon; bring to a boil and simmer for 10 minutes. Remove from heat; strain. If necessary, add water to make 1 cup.
Dissolve gelatin in boiling water. Stir in spiced peach syrup. Chill until slightly thickened. Fold in diced peaches. Pour into a 3-cup mold and chill until firm. Yield: 6 servings.

RED RASPBERRY RING

1 (10-ounce) package frozen red raspberries, thawed
1 (6-ounce) package red raspberry-flavored gelatin
2 cups boiling water
1 pint vanilla ice cream
1 (6-ounce) can frozen pink lemonade, undiluted
1/4 cup chopped pecans

Drain raspberries and set aside. Dissolve gelatin in boiling water; add ice cream by spoonfuls, stirring until melted. Stir in lemonade. Chill until partially set. Add raspberries and pecans. Put into a 6-cup ring mold. Chill until firm. Yield: 6 to 8 servings.

RED AND GREEN SALAD

1 (3-ounce) package lime-flavored gelatin
1 cup boiling water
1 (2-ounce) jar pimientos, drained and chopped
1 (3-ounce) package cream cheese, softened
1 (8 1/4-ounce) can crushed pineapple, undrained
1 cup finely chopped celery
1/2 pint whipping cream, stiffly whipped
Salad greens

Dissolve gelatin in boiling water; chill. Mix pimiento and cream cheese until smooth. When partially thickened, beat gelatin and add to cream cheese mixture. Fold in pineapple and celery. Have whipped cream very stiff before folding into gelatin mixture. Chill until firm. Serve on salad greens and garnish as desired. Yield: 12 servings.

TEA GARDEN SALAD

1 (3-ounce) package orange-flavored
 gelatin
1 cup medium-strength boiling tea
1 (11-ounce) can mandarin oranges,
 drained, liquid reserved
1 (8 1/4-ounce) can crushed pineapple,
 drained, liquid reserved
3/4 cup combined fruit liquids
1 (6-ounce) can water chestnuts,
 drained and sliced
 Mayonnaise
 Whipping cream, whipped
 Ground mace

Dissolve gelatin in boiling tea. Add
combined fruit liquids to gelatin mixture.
Stir and cool until mixture thickens
slightly. Add oranges, pineapple, and
water chestnuts. Spoon into a 6-cup mold
and chill until firm.

For the topping combine equal parts
mayonnaise and whipped cream, and add
a dash of mace. Yield: 8 servings.

MOLDED CHEESE SNOWCAP SALAD

1 (3-ounce) package orange-flavored
 gelatin
1 cup boiling water
1/2 cup cold water
1 1/2 cups small-curd creamed cottage
 cheese
2 (3-ounce) packages cream cheese,
 softened
1 cup seedless green grapes
1 cup finely chopped pecans
1/2 pint whipping cream, whipped
1 cup crushed pineapple, drained
 Maraschino cherries

Dissolve gelatin in boiling water; add
cold water and chill. Combine cottage
cheese and cream cheese; mash until well
blended. Stir into gelatin mixture. Stir in
grapes, pecans, whipped cream, and
pineapple. Pour into individual molds
and chill. Garnish each serving with a
maraschino cherry. Yield: 12 servings.

SALAD SUPREME

2 (3-ounce) packages orange-flavored
 gelatin
1 (20-ounce) can crushed pineapple,
 drained, liquid reserved
1 cup chopped walnuts, divided
1 (8-ounce) package whipped topping
 mix
1 (8-ounce) package cream cheese,
 softened
1 tablespoon lemon juice
3/4 cup sugar
2 tablespoons all-purpose flour
2 eggs, beaten

Prepare gelatin according to package
directions; chill until mixture begins to
congeal. Add pineapple to chilled gelatin;
pour into an oiled 13- x 9- x 2-inch pan.
Sprinkle with 1/2 cup walnuts; chill until
mixture is completely congealed.

Prepare whipped topping mix according
to package directions; blend in cream
cheese. Spread this mixture over congealed
gelatin; cover and chill.

Add enough water to reserved
pineapple liquid to make 1 cup. Combine
lemon juice, sugar, flour, and eggs; add to
pineapple liquid. Cook over low heat
until thickened; chill thoroughly. When
this mixture is cool, spread over cream
cheese mixture. Sprinkle remaining
walnuts on top. Chill. Yield: 12 to 15
servings.

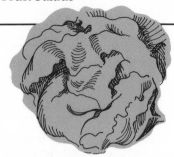

MARSHMALLOW-CHEESE DELIGHT SALAD

- 1 (3-ounce) package lemon-flavored gelatin
- 1 (3-ounce) package orange-flavored gelatin
- 2 cups boiling water
- 1/2 cup cold water
- 1 (20-ounce) can apricots, drained and quartered, liquid reserved
- 1 (13 1/2-ounce) can pineapple tidbits, drained, liquid reserved
- 3 cups miniature marshmallows
  Lettuce
  Pineapple Topping
- 1 cup dessert topping or 1/2 pint whipping cream, whipped
- 3/4 cup shredded Cheddar cheese

Dissolve gelatin in boiling water. Add cold water and apricot liquid. Chill until almost firm. Fold in fruits and marshmallows. Pour into a 2 1/2-quart mold. Chill until firm.

Unmold salad on lettuce, and spread with Pineapple Topping. Spread dessert topping or whipped cream over Pineapple Topping. Sprinkle with cheese. Yield: 10 to 12 servings.

Pineapple Topping:

- 2/3 cup reserved pineapple liquid
- 1 tablespoon all-purpose flour
- 1 egg, beaten

Combine liquid, flour, and egg; cook over low heat until thickened. Cool and chill. Spread over salad. Yield: 1 cup.

ORANGE MANDARIN SALAD

- 3 (3-ounce) packages orange-flavored gelatin
- 2 cups boiling water
- 1 pint orange sherbet
- 3 (11-ounce) cans mandarin oranges, undrained
  Topping

Dissolve gelatin in boiling water; add orange sherbet. Stir until melted. Add oranges and liquid. Pour into mold and chill. Serve with Topping. Yield: 10 to 12 servings.

Topping:

- 1 pint whipping cream, whipped
- 1 (3-ounce) package cream cheese, softened
- 1/2 cup marshmallow whip

Combine all ingredients. Yield: about 2 cups.

STRAWBERRY-PINEAPPLE SALAD

- 1 (3-ounce) package strawberry-flavored gelatin
- 3/4 cup boiling water
- 1 (10-ounce) package frozen strawberries
- 1 (8 1/4-ounce) can crushed pineapple, undrained
- 1 banana, mashed
- 1 cup commercial sour cream

Dissolve gelatin in boiling water. Cool; then add slightly thawed strawberries and pineapple. Chill until consistency of honey. Stir in banana. Spoon half this mixture into a loaf pan, spread sour cream over this layer, and top with another layer of gelatin mixture. Chill until firm. Yield: 8 to 10 servings.

Vegetable Salads

BLACK-EYED PEA SALAD

    1 cup mayonnaise
    1 tablespoon Worcestershire sauce
    1 teaspoon salt
    1 teaspoon pepper
  1/2 teaspoon Beau Monde seasoning
      Juice of 1 lemon
  1/2 teaspoon hot sauce
    2 tablespoons instant minced onion
    1 teaspoon instant minced garlic
2 1/2 (15-ounce) cans black-eyed peas,
      drained
      Lettuce
      Tomato and onion wedges

Combine first 9 ingredients; add peas.
Cover and chill overnight. Serve on
lettuce with tomato and onion wedges.
Yield: 6 to 8 servings.

MUSHROOM SALAD

    1 pound fresh mushrooms
  1/4 cup lemon juice
    6 tablespoons olive oil
    1 teaspoon salt
    2 teaspoons freshly ground black
      pepper
    1 tablespoon chopped parsley

Trim mushroom stems and wipe caps
with a damp cloth. Cut mushrooms into
thin T-shaped slices. Combine
mushrooms, lemon juice, oil, salt, and
pepper. Mix well; marinate at room
temperature for 1 hour; cover and chill for
1 hour before serving. Sprinkle with
parsley and serve. Yield: 8 servings.

HOT CURRIED SLAW

    1 large onion, finely diced
    2 tablespoons butter
  1/2 clove garlic
    2 teaspoons all-purpose flour
    2 teaspoons curry powder
    1 (10 1/2-ounce) can beef consommé
    1 can water
1 1/2 cups commercial sour cream
      Dash pepper
    4 whole cloves
    6 cups shredded cabbage

Brown onion in butter; add garlic and
blend in flour and curry powder.
Combine consommé and water; add 1 cup
of this to onion mixture. Remove garlic
clove and add sour cream. Simmer over
low heat until mixture thickens. Add
pepper and set aside.

Heat remaining beef consommé; add
cloves and cabbage. Cover pan and
simmer for 5 minutes. Remove cloves. Put
cabbage into a buttered casserole; add
onion and sauce mixture and mix well
with a fork. Bake at 350° for 20 minutes.
Yield: 6 servings.

STUFFED CUCUMBER-CHEESE SALAD

4 (8-inch) cucumbers
  Salt
3 (3-ounce) packages cream cheese, softened
2 tablespoons minced onion
3 tablespoons finely chopped green pepper
3 tablespoons finely chopped red pepper
1 teaspoon salt
1/8 teaspoon white pepper
1 teaspoon paprika
  Lettuce
  Tomato wedges
  Mayonnaise

Wash cucumbers, score with a fork, and cut in half, crosswise. Scoop out seeds, leaving centers hollow, and sprinkle inside with salt. Drain. Combine cream cheese, onion, green and red pepper, salt, white pepper, and paprika. Mix well and pack into the cucumber cavities. Wrap in foil. Chill several hours or overnight. Slice and serve on lettuce with tomato wedges and mayonnaise. If desired, slice cucumbers into thin slices and serve as hors d'oeuvres with fruit juice or cocktails. Yield: 8 servings.

MEXICAN POTATO SALAD

4 large unpeeled potatoes, cooked, drained, cooled, and diced
1 (1 3/8-ounce) package onion soup mix
1 cup commercial sour cream
1/2 cup chopped celery
1/4 cup chopped sweet pickle
2 hard-cooked eggs, chopped
1 pimiento, chopped
  Dash paprika
  Salt and pepper to taste

Combine first 8 ingredients and mix well. Season with salt and pepper. Chill well before serving. Yield: 6 to 8 servings.

SALAD NICOISE

1 small head iceberg lettuce, torn into bite-size pieces
1 head Boston lettuce, torn into bite-size pieces
2 cups cooked, cubed potatoes
1 (10-ounce) package frozen French-style green beans, cooked
1 (7-ounce) can white tuna fish, drained and flaked
1/4 green pepper, cut into strips
2 hard-cooked eggs, sliced
16 pitted ripe olives
1 small onion, thinly sliced
1 medium-size tomato, cut into 8 wedges
1 (0.84-ounce) package old-fashioned French dressing mix
2 tablespoons water
1/4 cup red wine vinegar
2/3 cup salad oil
1 tablespoon lemon juice
1 teaspoon seasoned salt
1/2 teaspoon seasoned pepper

Place lettuce in bottom of a very large salad bowl. Arrange potatoes, green beans, tuna fish, green pepper, eggs, olives, onion, and tomato in attractive pattern on lettuce.
Combine French dressing mix and water in a jar; shake well. Add vinegar and oil; shake again. When salad is ready to be served, toss it lightly with dressing, lemon juice, salt, and pepper. Yield: 6 to 8 servings.

SALADE DE TURQUIE

1/4 teaspoon instant minced garlic
1 tablespoon vinegar
2 teaspoons salt
1/2 teaspoon dillseeds (or 1 tablespoon snipped fresh dill)
1 3/4 cups plain yogurt
1 tablespoon olive oil
3 medium-size cucumbers, quartered, thinly sliced, and chilled
1 tablespoon snipped mint leaves
1 cup halved seedless green grapes (optional) or canned grapes, drained
Mint sprigs

An hour or two before serving, combine garlic, vinegar, salt, dillseeds, yogurt, and olive oil in a medium-size bowl; chill.

About 20 minutes before serving, combine yogurt mixture, cucumbers, snipped mint, and grapes; top with mint sprigs. Chill until served. Yield: 6 to 8 servings.

CUCUMBER-CHEESE SLAW

1 medium-size head cabbage, finely chopped
1/2 cup thinly sliced stuffed olives
1/2 teaspoon salt
1 tablespoon celery seeds
1/2 cup grated cucumber
1 (3-ounce) package cream cheese, softened
1/2 cup mayonnaise

Combine cabbage, olives, salt, celery seeds, and cucumber. Combine cream cheese and mayonnaise; beat until smooth. Chill cabbage mixture and cream cheese mixture; just before serving, combine them and toss lightly. Yield: 6 to 8 servings.

LUNCHEON SALAD ROMANOFF

1/2 cup cooked asparagus
1/2 cup cooked green beans
1/2 cup cooked green peas
4 radishes, sliced
2 artichoke hearts, chopped
2 hard-cooked eggs, chopped
1 teaspoon fresh mixed herbs
1/3 cup commercial French dressing
1/4 cup mayonnaise

Toss lightly all ingredients except mayonnaise, and marinate for at least 30 minutes, Before serving, blend in mayonnaise. Yield: 4 servings.

HAWAIIAN COLESLAW

1 (11-ounce) can mandarin oranges, drained, liquid reserved
1 tablespoon mandarin orange liquid
4 cups shredded cabbage
1/2 teaspoon salt
1/4 teaspoon ground ginger
1/4 teaspoon ground nutmeg
1/4 teaspoon white pepper
1 cup crushed pineapple, drained
1/2 cup mayonnaise or tart salad dressing

Combine mandarin orange liquid, cabbage, salt, spices, and pepper. Toss lightly. Add oranges and pineapple, tossing all with a fork. Stir in mayonnaise or salad dressing. Chill well before serving. Yield: 6 servings.

HOT FRESH APPLE SLAW

3 cups finely shredded cabbage
2 tablespoons cider vinegar
2 teaspoons sugar
2 tablespoons butter or margarine
1 teaspoon tarragon leaves
1/4 teaspoon salt
   Dash freshly ground black pepper
2 cups (2 medium-size) grated raw
   apples

Place cabbage, vinegar, sugar, butter or margarine, and seasonings in a saucepan. Bring to boiling point. Stir in apples and cook only to heat apples. Serve as meat accompaniment. This dish is especially good when served with pork, ham, corn beef, or tongue. Yield: 6 servings.

SCANDINAVIAN VEGETABLE SALAD

1 (16-ounce) can cut green beans,
   drained
1 (16-ounce) can English peas,
   drained
1 (16-ounce) can whole kernel corn,
   drained
2 cups chopped celery
1 (4-ounce) jar pimientos, chopped
1/2 cup chopped onion
   Salt to taste
1 cup sugar
1 1/2 tablespoons salt
1 cup vinegar
1/2 cup salad oil
1 teaspoon paprika

Combine vegetables and salt. Stir well and chill for 1 hour. Remove from refrigerator and drain again. Add remaining ingredients and stir until sugar is dissolved. Pour into a large dish, cover, and chill several hours. Yield: 8 to 10 servings.

CHINESE SLAW

1 (8-ounce) can French-style green
   beans, drained
1 (3-ounce) can sliced mushrooms,
   drained
1 diced pimiento
1 (16-ounce) can Chinese vegetables,
   drained
1 (8 1/2-ounce) can English peas,
   drained
1 (6-ounce) can water chestnuts,
   drained and sliced
1 1/2 cups diced celery
1 onion, sliced and ringed
3/4 cup sugar
3/4 cup vinegar
   Salt and pepper to taste
   Ac'cent

Combine all vegetables in glass container. Heat sugar and vinegar and pour over vegetables. Add salt and pepper and a dash of Ac'cent. Yield: 8 to 10 servings.

GOURMET POTATO SALAD

1 cup creamed cottage cheese
1 cup commercial sour cream
2 teaspoons prepared mustard
2 teaspoons seasoned salt
4 cups cooked, sliced potatoes
1 cup sliced green onions with tops
1 cup sliced celery
1/2 cup diced green pepper
3 hard-cooked eggs, chopped
1 (1-ounce) package blue cheese,
   crumbled

Combine cottage cheese, sour cream, mustard, and salt. Pour over potatoes, onions, celery, green pepper, and eggs; mix carefully. Chill several hours to blend flavors. Fold in blue cheese just before serving. Yield: 6 to 8 servings.

FRESH SNAP BEAN SALAD, ITALIAN STYLE

2 cups cooked fresh green beans
2 cups cooked, diced potatoes
1/4 cup chopped onion
1/8 teaspoon minced fresh garlic
1 teaspoon salt
1/8 teaspoon freshly ground black pepper
2 tablespoons salad oil
1 cup diced celery
8 anchovies, diced
3 tablespoons mayonnaise
1 tablespoon cider vinegar
Head lettuce
Black olives

Combine the first 7 ingredients; mix lightly. Cover and marinate in the refrigerator for at least 1 hour. Just before serving, add celery, anchovies, mayonnaise, and vinegar. Mix lightly. Serve on lettuce and garnish with black olives. Yield: 8 servings.

DELICIOUS COLESLAW

1/2 cup evaporated milk
1/2 cup mayonnaise
1/2 teaspoon hot sauce
6 tablespoons vinegar
2 teaspoons prepared mustard
1 tablespoon sugar
1/2 teaspoon celery seeds
1 1/2 teaspoons salt
10 cups shredded cabbage
1 cup shredded carrots
2/3 cup finely chopped green pepper

Combine evaporated milk and mayonnaise; blend until smooth. Stir in hot sauce, vinegar, mustard, sugar, celery seeds, and salt. Put cabbage, carrots, and green pepper into large bowl; pour dressing over and toss gently. Yield: 12 servings.

FALL GARDEN SALAD TRAY

2 medium-size carrots, pared, cut into 3-inch sticks, cooked, and drained
1/2 cup cooked lima beans, drained
1 cup cooked cut green beans, drained
1 cup whole mushrooms
Commercial Italian dressing
1/2 large cucumber, scored and thinly sliced
1/2 large sweet onion, thinly sliced and ringed
1/4 cup vinegar
1/4 cup water
1 teaspoon salt
1 cup pickled beets, chilled

Place carrots, limas, green beans, and mushrooms in separate piles in a shallow dish. Pour Italian dressing over vegetables and chill for 1 hour.
Pile cucumbers and onions in separate stacks in a shallow dish. Add dressing made from vinegar, water, and salt, well blended. Chill for 1 hour.
Arrange vegetables on a tray and add beets at serving time. Yield: 8 servings.

SAUERKRAUT SALAD

1 (27-ounce) can chopped sauerkraut
1 large onion, chopped
1 cup chopped celery
1 green pepper, chopped
1 (2-ounce) jar pimiento, chopped
1 1/4 cups sugar

Combine all ingredients except sugar; sprinkle sugar over top of mixture. Cover container and chill for 24 hours. Mix well and serve. Yield: 6 servings.

TEXAS COLESLAW

    1 cup sugar
    1 large cabbage, shredded
    1 large onion, thinly sliced
  2/3 cup salad oil
    1 cup wine vinegar
    1 tablespoon celery seeds
    1 tablespoon dry mustard

Sprinkle sugar over cabbage and onion; mix well. Combine oil, vinegar, celery seeds, and dry mustard in saucepan; bring to a boil, stirring constantly. Pour hot sauce over cabbage-onion mixture and toss well. Cover; refrigerate at least 8 hours. Yield: 8 servings.

GERMAN POTATO SALAD

  1/2 cup salad oil
    1 cup cider vinegar
1 1/2 cups water
    1 heaping teaspoon all-purpose flour
    1 teaspoon salt
    1 tablespoon sugar
    2 tablespoons celery seeds
    2 onions, chopped
   12 potatoes, boiled, peeled, cooled,
        and sliced
        Hard-cooked eggs

Combine salad oil, vinegar, water, and flour in saucepan; boil until slightly thickened. Remove from heat and add salt, sugar, celery seeds, and onions. Spoon this mixture over potatoes. Serve either hot or cold. This salad is even better if allowed to sit overnight in covered dish in refrigerator. Garnish with hard-cooked eggs. Yield: 12 to 15 servings.

DEVILED POTATO SALAD

    8 hard-cooked eggs
    2 tablespoons vinegar
    1 tablespoon prepared horseradish
2 1/2 tablespoons prepared mustard
    1 cup mayonnaise or salad dressing
    1 cup commercial sour cream
  1/2 teaspoon celery salt
    1 teaspoon salt
4 1/2 cups (6 medium-size) potatoes,
        boiled, peeled, and cubed
    1 cup chopped celery
  1/4 cup chopped onion
    2 tablespoons chopped green pepper
    2 tablespoons chopped pimiento
        Tomato wedges
        Cucumber slices

Cut eggs in half and remove yolks. Mash and blend yolks with vinegar, horseradish, and mustard. Add mayonnaise or salad dressing, sour cream, celery salt, and salt; mix well. Chop egg whites; combine with potatoes, celery, onion, green pepper, and pimiento. Fold in egg yolk mixture; chill. Garnish with tomato wedges and cucumber slices. Yield: 6 to 8 servings.

PIQUANT MUSHROOMS

    1 (4-ounce) can whole button
        mushrooms, drained
    2 tablespoons chopped onion
    2 tablespoons salad oil
    1 teaspoon vinegar
  1/2 teaspoon lemon juice
  1/2 teaspoon sugar
        Dash salt

Combine mushrooms and onion. To make dressing, combine remaining ingredients and mix well. Pour dressing over mushrooms. Chill. Yield: 4 to 6 servings.

CONFETTI ARTICHOKES

1 (9-ounce) package frozen artichoke
   hearts, cooked and drained
2 tablespoons chopped pimiento
1/4 cup commercial Italian dressing
1/8 teaspoon salt
   Dash pepper

Mix ingredients and toss to combine
flavors. Chill. Yield: 4 to 6 servings.

HOT PINEAPPLE-YAM SALAD

6 1-inch slices bacon, crisply fried,
   drippings reserved
2 tablespoons bacon drippings
1/3 cup chopped onion
1/2 cup thinly sliced celery
2 tablespoons chopped green pepper
1/4 teaspoon dry mustard
1/2 teaspoon salt
1 teaspoon all-purpose flour
1 (13 1/4-ounce) can pineapple tidbits,
   drained, liquid reserved
1/4 cup pineapple liquid
1 tablespoon cider vinegar
1 pound yams, boiled, cooled, peeled,
   and sliced

Keep bacon warm. Sauté onion, celery,
and green pepper in bacon drippings.
Add mustard, salt, flour, pineapple
liquid, and vinegar. Cook a few minutes
and add pineapple tidbits. Cover and
keep warm. Combine yams with
pineapple mixture, tossing lightly to mix.
Top with crumbled bacon and serve hot.
Yield: 6 servings.

THREE BEAN SALAD

1 (16-ounce) can cut green beans,
   drained
1 (16-ounce) can cut yellow wax beans,
   drained
1 (16-ounce) can red kidney beans,
   drained
1/4 cup chopped green pepper
1 medium-size onion, thinly sliced
1/2 cup cider vinegar
1/3 cup salad oil
1/2 cup sugar
1 teaspoon salt
1 teaspoon pepper

Rinse beans well, and drain again. Add
green pepper and onion to beans. Mix
other ingredients and add to bean
mixture. Mix well and chill overnight.
Yield: 10 to 12 servings.

TOMATO SURPRISE SALAD

6 medium-size tomatoes, scalded and
   peeled
1/2 cup cooked, diced chicken
1/2 cup diced celery
1/4 cup chopped nuts
1 tablespoon grated onion
1/4 cup mayonnaise
   Salt to taste

Carefully scoop out the inside of
tomatoes; chill cases. Mix tomato pulp
with chicken, celery, nuts, onion, and
mayonnaise; add salt, if needed. Fill
tomatoes with chicken mixture and serve
cold. Yield: 6 servings.

POTLUCK POTATO SALAD

1/3 cup commercial French dressing
  6 large potatoes, cooked, peeled, and
     cubed
1 1/4 cups chopped celery
1/3 cup chopped onion
  5 hard-cooked eggs, chopped
1 1/2 teaspoons salt
  1 cup mayonnaise
     Cherry tomatoes (optional)

Pour French dressing over potatoes.
Chill about 2 hours. Add remaining
ingredients except tomatoes and mix
lightly. Chill. Garnish with cherry
tomatoes, if desired. Yield: 8 to 10
servings.

POTATO SALAD IN TOMATO CUPS

  2 cups cooked, pared, and sliced
     potatoes
1/3 cup finely chopped celery
1/3 cup chopped radishes
1/4 cup chopped green onions with tops
1/4 cup sweet pickle relish
1/2 teaspoon salt
1/2 teaspoon celery salt
1/8 teaspoon pepper
1/2 cup salad dressing or mayonnaise
  2 teaspoons prepared mustard
  2 hard-cooked eggs, chopped
  6 chilled tomatoes
     Salt

Combine potatoes, celery, radishes,
green onions, pickle relish, salt, celery
salt, and pepper in a large bowl. Stir
together salad dressing or mayonnaise
and mustard; spoon over potato mixture
and toss lightly. Carefully stir in eggs.
Cover; chill thoroughly. At serving time,
cut out core of chilled tomatoes. Cut each
tomato into sixths, cutting to within 1/2
inch of bottom. Carefully spread out

sections to form a cup, sprinkle with salt,
and fill with potato salad. Yield: 6
servings.

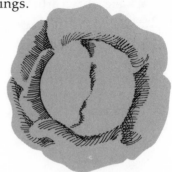

BEET AND HORSERADISH SALAD

1 (16-ounce) can tiny whole beets,
   drained, liquid reserved
6 tablespoons horseradish
4 teaspoons sugar
4 teaspoons vinegar
   Salt and pepper to taste

Heat beet liquid with horseradish,
sugar, vinegar, salt, and pepper. Pour
over beets and chill until ready to serve.
Yield: 4 to 6 servings.

POTATO SALAD AMANDINE

  6 medium-size potatoes, cooked,
     peeled, and sliced
  1 medium-size onion, chopped
1/2 cup toasted slivered almonds
  2 tablespoons chopped parsley
  2 tablespoons salad oil
  6 tablespoons vinegar
  2 teaspoons salt
1/2 teaspoon sugar
1/4 teaspoon paprika

Combine potatoes, onion, almonds,
and parsley in medium-size bowl. Mix
remaining ingredients; pour over potato
mixture. Toss lightly to mix. Cover and
chill several hours to blend flavors. Yield:
4 servings.

LETTUCE CUP SALAD

  4 hard-cooked eggs
  2 tablespoons mayonnaise
  1 (2 1/4-ounce) can deviled ham
  2 cups chopped cabbage
1/2 cup grated carrots
1/2 cup salad dressing or mayonnaise
  4 lettuce cups
1/4 cup chopped chives

Split hard-cooked eggs; remove yolks and blend with 2 tablespoons mayonnaise and deviled ham. Stuff egg halves with mixture.

Mix cabbage, carrots, and salad dressing or mayonnaise; place in lettuce cups. Top each with 2 ham-stuffed egg halves, and garnish with chives. Yield: 4 servings.

CABBAGE AND PEANUT SALAD

  1 egg
1/2 cup vinegar
1/2 cup water
  1 teaspoon salt
1/2 teaspoon dry mustard
  2 tablespoons sugar
  2 cups finely shredded cabbage
1/2 cup chopped peanuts
1/2 teaspoon celery seeds

Beat egg in small saucepan. Add vinegar, water, salt, dry mustard, and sugar. Mix thoroughly and cook over low heat, beating constantly until mixture is slightly thickened. Cool. Pour dressing mixture over combined cabbage, peanuts, and celery seeds. Yield: 4 to 6 servings.

APPLE-SOUR CREAM SLAW

  1 cup sliced celery
  2 cups shredded cabbage
  1 cup shredded carrots
  2 large red apples, diced
1/3 cup seedless raisins
1/3 cup chopped salted peanuts
  1 cup commercial sour cream
  2 tablespoons lemon juice
  2 tablespoons cider vinegar
  2 tablespoons sugar
  1 teaspoon salt
1/4 teaspoon pepper
  1 teaspoon dry mustard

Combine celery, cabbage, carrots, apples, raisins, and peanuts. Mix remaining ingredients to make a dressing and pour over vegetable mixture. Toss to mix well. Yield: 10 to 12 servings.

CLUB COLESLAW

  1 (2-pound) head cabbage, shredded
  1 green pepper, diced
  1 red pepper, diced
  1 (13 1/4-ounce) can pineapple tidbits, drained
1/4 cup sugar
  1 teaspoon salt
  1 cup mayonnaise
  2 tablespoons lemon, lime, or orange juice
1/2 teaspoon dry mustard
  1 teaspoon celery seeds

Combine cabbage, peppers, and pineapple. Sprinkle with sugar and salt; stir to mix. Let stand about 30 minutes.

Combine mayonnaise, citrus juice, and dry mustard; stir into cabbage mixture. At serving time, sprinkle with celery seeds. Yield: 12 servings.

CUCUMBER COLESLAW

4 cups shredded cabbage
2 cups peeled, diced cucumber
1 medium-size onion, thinly sliced and soaked in vinegar
1 teaspoon sugar
1/2 teaspoon salt
1/2 teaspoon celery seeds
1 tablespoon tarragon vinegar
1/2 cup salad dressing or mayonnaise

Combine cabbage and cucumber; add onion and toss. Sprinkle sugar and salt over mixture. Add celery seeds and tarragon vinegar; mix well. Add salad dressing or mayonnaise and mix well. Yield: 6 servings.

TOMATO-COTTAGE CHEESE SALAD

1 medium-size tomato
2 green pepper rings (1/8 inch thick)
4 tablespoons dry or creamed cottage cheese
2 large lettuce leaves
1 hard-cooked egg, sliced
2 carrot curls
1 small radish

Slice tomato in thirds and alternate with rings of green pepper, spooning 2 tablespoons cottage cheese between each. Hold together with wooden picks. Place on lettuce leaves and garnish with egg, carrot curls, and radish. Yield: 1 serving.

CRISP WINTER SALAD

1 tablespoon lemon juice
1/4 cup mayonnaise or salad dressing
1/2 cup coarsely grated raw rutabaga
1 cup shredded cabbage
1 cup unpeeled diced red apples
1/4 cup seedless raisins
1/4 cup chopped peanuts

Combine lemon juice and mayonnaise or salad dressing. Toss remaining ingredients together. Top with dressing mixture. Yield: 4 servings.

TROPICAL SALAD AND DRESSING

4 cups hearts of palm or lettuce
1 cup pineapple chunks, drained, liquid reserved
1/4 cup chopped dates
1/4 cup candied or preserved ginger, chopped, drained, and liquid reserved (optional)
4 tablespoons vanilla ice cream
2 tablespoons mayonnaise
2 tablespoons crunchy peanut butter

Combine first 4 ingredients.
Mix ice cream, mayonnaise, and peanut butter thoroughly; thin with either pineapple or ginger liquid, if desired. Pour over salad and serve. Yield: 6 servings.

SCANDINAVIAN SALAD

6 potatoes, boiled, peeled, and diced
Commercial French dressing
1 (5-ounce) jar pickled herring, cut into chunks
2 apples, peeled and diced
3 hard-cooked eggs, chopped
1/4 teaspoon tarragon
Salt and pepper to taste
1/3 cup mayonnaise
1 (16-ounce) can diced beets, drained well
Capers

Sprinkle potatoes lightly with French dressing. Let cool. Add herring, apples, eggs, seasonings, and mayonnaise. Mix well. Just before serving, stir in beets. Garnish with capers. Yield: 4 to 6 servings.

Molded Vegetable Salads

TOMATO-CREAM CHEESE SALAD

        1 (10 3/4-ounce) can tomato soup,
           undiluted
  1 1/2 envelopes (1 1/2 tablespoons)
           unflavored gelatin
    1/2 cup cold water
        2 (3-ounce) packages cream cheese,
           softened
        1 cup chopped celery
    1/2 cup stuffed olives, sliced
    1/2 teaspoon onion juice
        1 cup chopped pecans (optional)

   Heat tomato soup. Stir in gelatin, which
has been softened in 1/2 cup cold water;
stir until gelatin dissolves. Cool slightly;
then stir in other ingredients. Put into an
oiled 5-cup mold and chill until firm.
Yield: 6 to 8 servings.

MOLDED BEET SALAD

       1 envelope (1 tablespoon) unflavored
          gelatin
   1/4 cup cold water
   3/4 cup diced beets, drained, liquid
          reserved
       1 cup mandarin oranges, drained,
          liquid reserved
   1/4 teaspoon salt
       3 tablespoons minced onion
   1/4 cup vinegar or lemon juice
          Lettuce
          Mayonnaise
          Celery salt

   Soften gelatin in cold water for 5
minutes. Combine beet and orange liquid
and add enough water to make 1 1/4 cups.
Heat liquid to boiling and add gelatin;
then add salt, onion, and vinegar or
lemon juice (or combination of the two).
Chill. When mixture is slightly thickened,
fold in beets and oranges. Pour into 6
individual molds and chill until firm.
Unmold on lettuce and serve with
mayonnaise with dash of celery salt.
Yield: 6 servings.

CARROT-PINEAPPLE SALAD

       2 (3-ounce) packages lemon-flavored
          gelatin
       2 cups boiling water
       1 (19 1/2-ounce) can crushed pineapple,
          drained, liquid reserved
       1 cup grated carrots
       1 cup shredded Cheddar cheese
   3/4 cup chopped pecans

   Dissolve gelatin in boiling water. Add
enough water to pineapple liquid to make
2 cups and stir into gelatin. Refrigerate
until partially congealed; stir in
pineapple, carrots, cheese, and pecans.
Pour into a 2 1/2-quart mold or individual
molds. Chill until firm. Yield: 12 servings.

PLANTATION SALAD

    4 envelopes (4 tablespoons)
      unflavored gelatin
    1 cup cold water
  1/2 cup vinegar
    4 tablespoons lemon juice
  1/2 cup sugar
  1/2 teaspoon salt
4 1/2 cups boiling water
    4 cups shredded cabbage
    3 cups diced pineapple
  1/2 cup chopped green pepper
  1/2 cup chopped pimiento

   Soften gelatin in cold water; add
vinegar, lemon juice, sugar, salt, and
boiling water. Stir until gelatin is
dissolved; chill until syrupy. Combine
cabbage, pineapple, green pepper, and
pimiento; stir into gelatin mixture. Pour
into two 2-quart ring molds. Chill until
firm. Yield: 25 servings.

CONGEALED CARROT SALAD

    2 envelopes (2 tablespoons)
      unflavored gelatin
1 1/2 cups cold orange juice, divided
  1/2 cup boiling orange juice
  1/4 teaspoon salt
    1 cup salad dressing or mayonnaise
1 1/2 cups finely grated carrots
    1 (13 1/4-ounce) can crushed
      pineapple, drained

   Dissolve gelatin in 1/2 cup cold orange
juice. Add to boiling orange juice and stir
until gelatin dissolves. Add remaining 1
cup of cold orange juice. Stir in salt, salad
dressing or mayonnaise, carrots, and
pineapple. Pour into a 6-cup mold and
chill until firm, stirring several times to
prevent carrots from settling to bottom.
Yield: 8 servings.

SPICY BEET SALAD

    1 (3-ounce) package lemon-flavored
      gelatin
    1 cup boiling water
  1/2 teaspoon salt
    3 tablespoons vinegar
    1 (16-ounce) can diced beets, drained,
      liquid reserved
  3/4 cup beet liquid
1 1/2 cups finely chopped cabbage
1 1/2 teaspoons freshly grated
      horseradish

   Dissolve gelatin in boiling water; stir in
salt, vinegar, and beet liquid. Chill until
slightly thickened. Stir in beets, cabbage,
and horseradish. Pour into a 5-cup mold
and chill until firm. Yield: 6 servings.

CARDINAL SALAD

    1 (3-ounce) package lemon-flavored
      gelatin
    1 cup boiling water
    1 cup diced cooked beets, drained,
      liquid reserved
  3/4 cup beet liquid
    2 tablespoons vinegar
    2 tablespoons lemon juice
  1/8 teaspoon salt
  3/4 teaspoon freshly grated horseradish
      or onion
  1/2 cup diced celery
      Salad greens

   Dissolve gelatin in boiling water; add
beet liquid, vinegar, lemon juice, salt, and
horseradish or onion. Chill until slightly
thickened. Fold in beets and celery. Pour
into a 4-cup mold and chill until firm.
Unmold on salad greens. Yield: 6
servings.

CHEESE-TOMATO ASPIC PLATTER

Cheese-Olive Layer:

- 1 **envelope (1 tablespoon) unflavored gelatin**
- 1 **cup milk**
- 1/2 **teaspoon salt**
- 2 **teaspoons instant minced onion**
- 2 **(3-ounce) packages cream cheese, softened**
- 3/4 **cup salad dressing or mayonnaise**
- 2 **tablespoons lemon juice**
- 1 **teaspoon Worcestershire sauce**
- 1 **cup sliced stuffed olives**

Sprinkle gelatin over milk in saucepan. Place over low heat, and stir constantly until gelatin dissolves, about 3 to 4 minutes. Remove from heat; stir in salt and onion. Blend cream cheese and salad dressing or mayonnaise until smooth; stir in lemon juice and Worcestershire sauce. Gradually stir gelatin mixture into cream cheese mixture; beat, if necessary, until smooth. Chill, stirring occasionally, until mixture mounds slightly when dropped from spoon. Fold in sliced olives and turn into a 9- x 5- x 3-inch loaf pan or 2-quart mold. Chill until almost firm.

Tomato Aspic Layer:

- 3 **envelopes (3 tablespoons) unflavored gelatin**
- 2 **cups cold water, divided**
- 3 **(8-ounce) cans tomato sauce**
- 1 **tablespoon Worcestershire sauce**
- 1/4 **teaspoon hot sauce**
- 1 **tablespoon lemon juice**
  Salad greens

Sprinkle gelatin over 1 1/2 cups cold water in a 2 1/2-quart saucepan. Place over low heat; stir constantly until gelatin dissolves, about 2 to 3 minutes. Remove from heat; stir in remaining 1/2 cup cold water, tomato sauce, Worcestershire

sauce, hot sauce, and lemon juice. Cool, if necessary, to room temperature. Pour over almost-firm Cheese-Olive Layer. Chill until firm. Unmold on serving platter. Serve with salad greens. Yield: 8 servings.

TOMATO ASPIC WITH BLUE CHEESE TOPPING

- 3 **envelopes (3 tablespoons) unflavored gelatin**
- 1 **(46-ounce) can tomato juice, divided**
- 2 **tablespoons grated onion**
- 1/2 **teaspoon salt**
- 1 **cup chopped green pepper**
- 1 **cup chopped celery**
  Blue Cheese Topping

Soften gelatin in 1 1/2 cups tomato juice at room temperature; heat to dissolve gelatin. While warm, add onion, remainder of tomato juice, and salt. Chill until slightly thickened. Add green pepper and celery. Pour into prepared mold and chill until firm. Serve Blue Cheese Topping with salad. Yield: 10 to 12 servings.

Blue Cheese Topping:

- 1 **(3-ounce) package cream cheese, softened**
- 3 **tablespoons milk**
- 1 **(3-ounce) package blue cheese, crumbled**

Blend cream cheese and milk until the consistency of thick cream. With electric mixer, blend in blue cheese and whip until firm. Yield: 1 cup.

WONDER SALAD

- 1 (3-ounce) package lemon-flavored gelatin
- 1 (3-ounce) package lime-flavored gelatin
- 4 cups boiling water
- 1 envelope (1 tablespoon) unflavored gelatin
- 1/4 cup cold water
- 2 cups shredded cabbage
- 2 medium-size cucumbers, diced
- 2 tablespoons vinegar
  Juice of 1 lemon
- 1 (15 1/4-ounce) can crushed pineapple, well drained
- 1 cup chopped almonds
- 1 teaspoon salt

Dissolve flavored gelatin in boiling water. Dissolve unflavored gelatin in cold water; add to hot gelatin and stir until dissolved. Add other ingredients and chill until congealed. Yield: 10 servings.

POTATO SALAD MOLD

- 1 envelope (1 tablespoon) unflavored gelatin
- 1/4 cup cold water
- 1 (4 1/2-ounce) bottle stuffed olives, chopped, drained, liquid reserved
- 1/2 cup olive juice
- 1 cup chopped dill pickles, drained, liquid reserved
- 1/4 cup dill pickle juice
- 1/2 cup vinegar
- 20 medium-size potatoes, boiled, peeled, cooled, and chopped
- 2 medium-size onions, chopped
- 2 large green peppers, chopped
- 2 celery stalks, chopped
- 3/4 cup mayonnaise

Dissolve gelatin in cold water. Combine olive juice, pickle juice, and vinegar; bring to a boil and stir into gelatin. Chill until slightly congealed. Combine olives, pickles, potatoes, onions, green pepper, and celery. Add gelatin preparation and blend in mayonnaise. Put salad into mold and chill overnight. Yield: 20 servings.

RHUBARB SALAD

- 1 (10-ounce) package frozen rhubarb
- 2 to 4 tablespoons sugar
- 2 cups unsweetened pineapple juice
- 1 (6-ounce) package raspberry-flavored gelatin
- 2 cups peeled and chopped tart apples
- 1 cup chopped pecans

Cook rhubarb as directed on package. Sweeten to taste. Add pineapple juice and bring to a boil. Add gelatin and stir until dissolved. Chill until partially set; add apples and pecans.

Mix well and pour into molds. Chill overnight. Yield: 12 servings.

CUCUMBER SALAD

- 1 (3-ounce) package lime-flavored gelatin
- 3/4 cup hot water
- 1/4 cup lemon juice
- 1 teaspoon onion juice
- 1 cup commercial sour cream
  Lettuce
  Tomato wedges

Dissolve gelatin in hot water; add lemon juice and onion juice. Chill until partially set. Fold in sour cream and cucumber. Pour into oiled mold and chill until firm. Unmold and serve on lettuce-lined plate. Garnish with tomato wedges. Yield: 4 to 6 servings.

VEGETABLE SALAD MOLD

1 envelope (1 tablespoon) unflavored
  gelatin
3/4 cup cold water, divided
1 (3-ounce) package lime-flavored
  gelatin
1 cup boiling water
2 tablespoons vinegar
2 teaspoons grated onion
1 cup finely shredded sharp cheese
1/4 cup diced celery
1/2 cup sliced stuffed olives
  Dash salt

Dissolve unflavored gelatin in 1/4 cup cold water. Dissolve lime gelatin in boiling water; add unflavored gelatin and stir until dissolved. Add remaining 1/2 cup cold water and vinegar; chill until partially set. Stir in other ingredients and spoon into a 1-quart mold. Chill until firm. Yield: 6 servings.

WILLIAMSBURG INN SALAD

2 envelopes (2 tablespoons) unflavored
  gelatin
1 cup cold water, divided
1 cup boiling water
1/2 cup vinegar
1/2 teaspoon salt
2 cups sugar
  Few drops green food coloring
1 cup diced, blanched almonds
1 cup sliced sweet pickles
1 cup crushed pineapple, drained
1 cup sliced stuffed olives

Soften gelatin in 1/2 cup cold water; add boiling water and stir until dissolved. Add remaining 1/2 cup cold water, vinegar, salt, sugar, and green food coloring. Chill until mixture thickens. Fold in remaining ingredients. Chill until ready to serve. Yield: 6 servings.

BEET AND PINEAPPLE SALAD SUPREME

1 (3-ounce) package strawberry-
  flavored gelatin
1 (3-ounce) package raspberry-flavored
  gelatin
1 (3-ounce) package cherry-flavored
  gelatin
4 cups boiling water
1 (16-ounce) can French-cut beets,
  drained, liquid reserved
1 (20-ounce) can crushed pineapple,
  drained, liquid reserved
1/2 cup sweet pickle juice or vinegar
  Dressing

Dissolve all gelatins in boiling water. Combine reserved liquids from beets and pineapple (about 1 1/2 cups), and add with pickle juice to gelatin mixture. Chill until syrupy; stir in beets and pineapple. Put into a 2 1/2-quart mold and chill until firm. Serve with Dressing. Yield: 16 servings.

Dressing:

1 cup mayonnaise
1 tablespoon chopped green onion with
  top
1 tablespoon diced celery
1 tablespoon finely chopped green
  pepper
  Half-and-half (optional)

Mix first 4 ingredients and let stand several hours. Thin with half-and-half, if desired. Yield: about 1 1/4 cups.

LETTUCE-SHRIMP ASPIC MOLD

  2 envelopes (2 tablespoons) unflavored
    gelatin
3/4 teaspoon salt
  1 cup cold water
  2 cups tomato juice
  3 tablespoons lemon juice
  1 tablespoon grated onion
    Few dashes hot sauce
  1 head iceberg lettuce, cored, rinsed,
    drained, and chilled
  1 (5-ounce) can deveined shrimp,
    rinsed and drained
1/3 cup finely chopped dill pickle

Soften gelatin and salt in cold water; stir over medium heat until gelatin is completely dissolved. Stir in tomato juice, lemon juice, onion, and hot sauce. Chill until mixture begins to thicken.

Cut lettuce lengthwise into halves and shred across heart to make 1 quart. Chill all but 2 cups of shredded lettuce in plastic bag.

Fold 2 cups lettuce, shrimp, and pickle into gelatin mixture; turn into a 5-cup mold and chill until firm. Unmold on platter; arrange remaining shredded lettuce around edge of mold. Yield: 6 servings.

COOL-AS-A-CUCUMBER RING

  1 envelope (1 tablespoon) unflavored
    gelatin
1/2 cup cold water
1/2 teaspoon salt
  1 large cucumber, pared
1/2 small onion
  3 cups creamed cottage cheese
  1 (8-ounce) package cream cheese,
    softened
1/2 cup mayonnaise
2/3 cup chopped celery
1/3 cup nuts

Soften gelatin in water; add salt; heat and stir over low heat until gelatin is dissolved.

Cut cucumber in half and remove seeds; grate cucumber with onion and set aside. Beat the cheeses, and stir in gelatin. Add remaining ingredients. Pour into a 1-quart ring mold and chill overnight. Yield: 8 servings.

FIESTA GUACAMOLD

1/2 cup cold water
  2 envelopes (2 tablespoons)
    unflavored gelatin
1/2 cup boiling water
  2 large avocados, peeled and cut into
    pieces
  3 tablespoons lemon juice
  1 cup commercial sour cream
1 1/2 teaspoons salt
  1 teaspoon chili powder
1/4 teaspoon hot sauce
    Salad greens

Put cold water and gelatin into blender. Cover and process on low (stir) to soften gelatin; add boiling water. If gelatin granules cling to the container, scrape sides of container with a rubber spatula. When gelatin has dissolved, turn control to high (liquefy); add remaining ingredients, except salad greens, and continue to process until smooth and well blended. Pour into a 4-cup mold and chill until firm. Serve on salad greens. Yield: 8 servings.

DILL PICKLE SALAD

1 1/2 envelopes (1 1/2 tablespoons)
     unflavored gelatin
   1 cup cold water
   1 cup sugar
 1/4 cup lemon juice
 1/4 teaspoon salt
   2 dill pickles, chopped, drained,
     liquid reserved
 1/4 cup dill pickle juice
   1 cup crushed pineapple, drained,
     liquid reserved
 1/4 cup pineapple liquid
 1/2 cup pimientos, drained, liquid
     reserved
 1/4 cup pimiento liquid
   1 cup chopped pecans

Dissolve gelatin in cold water. Combine sugar, lemon juice, salt, pickle liquid, pineapple liquid, and pimiento liquid; bring to a boil and stir into gelatin. Cool. Chill until slightly congealed. Add pickles, pineapple, pimientos, and pecans. Pour into a 1 1/2-quart mold. Yield: 8 servings.

CUCUMBER CROWN SALAD

   1 (3-ounce) package lemon-flavored
     gelatin
1 3/4 cups apple juice, heated
   2 tablespoons lemon juice
 1/4 cup mayonnaise
   1 cup grated carrots
 1/4 cup diced celery
 1/4 cup peeled and diced cucumber
     Pinch salt
     Tomato slices
     Asparagus spears

Dissolve gelatin in hot apple juice; chill. When gelatin mixture begins to congeal, add lemon juice and mayonnaise; mix well. Add carrots, celery, cucumber, and salt; mix well. Pour into a 5-cup mold. Chill until firm. Unmold and garnish with tomato slices and asparagus spears. Yield: 6 servings.

SPRING BEAUTY SALAD

 1/4 cup all-purpose flour
 1/2 teaspoon salt
   2 teaspoons dry mustard
1 1/3 envelopes (1 tablespoon plus 1
     teaspoon) unflavored gelatin
   2 cups milk
 1/2 cup mayonnaise or salad dressing
 1/4 cup finely crumbled blue cheese
   1 cup finely diced cucumber
 1/4 cup thin green pepper strips
 1/4 cup thin pimiento strips
   2 tablespoons minced onion
     Salad greens
     Asparagus spears, cooked and
     wrapped in ham slices
     Radish roses
     Celery
     Carrot sticks

Combine flour, salt, mustard, and gelatin in heavy saucepan; gradually stir in milk. Cook and stir over low heat until sauce is thick and smooth. Cool until slightly thickened; then add mayonnaise or salad dressing and blend well. Fold in cheese, cucumber, green pepper, pimiento, and onion.

Pour into a 3 1/2-cup mold or 6 individual molds and chill until firm. Unmold on a salad plate and garnish with salad greens, asparagus spears, radish roses, celery, and carrot sticks. Yield: 6 servings.

DEVILISH EGG TREAT

1/4 cup cold water
  1 envelope (1 tablespoon) unflavored
     gelatin
1/2 cup boiling water
1/2 cup mayonnaise
3/4 teaspoon salt
1/4 teaspoon hot sauce
1/4 green pepper, diced
  1 cup diced celery
  4 hard-cooked eggs, quartered

Put cold water and gelatin into blender; cover and blend at low speed to soften. Add boiling water and continue to blend until gelatin is dissolved. If gelatin granules cling to container, scrape sides of container with a rubber spatula. Turn to high speed and add mayonnaise, salt, and hot sauce. Turn off blender and add remaining ingredients. Cover and chop by setting on high speed and turning on and off quickly several times. Pour into a 3-cup mold. Chill until firm. Yield: 4 to 6 servings.

CONGEALED CABBAGE SALAD

  1 (3-ounce) package lime-flavored
     gelatin
1 1/2 cups boiling water
  1 cup shredded cabbage
  1 cup shredded pasteurized process
     American cheese
  1 cup chopped pecans
  1 cup mayonnaise
     Dash salt

Dissolve gelatin in boiling water. Chill until partially set. Add cabbage, cheese, pecans, mayonnaise, and salt; mix well. Spoon into a 1 1/2-quart mold and chill until firm. Yield: 8 servings.

CARROT AND COLESLAW SALAD

  1 (3-ounce) package lemon-flavored
     gelatin
  1 cup hot water
1/2 cup cold water
  2 tablespoons vinegar
1/2 cup mayonnaise or salad dressing
1/4 teaspoon salt
1/4 teaspoon pepper
  1 cup shredded carrots
  1 cup shredded cabbage
  1 green pepper, finely chopped
1/2 onion, finely chopped
     Lettuce cups

Dissolve gelatin in hot water. Add cold water, vinegar, mayonnaise or salad dressing, salt, and pepper. Stir until well blended. Chill until partially set.

Beat chilled mixture and add carrots, cabbage, green pepper, and onion. Chill until firm. Serve in lettuce cups. Yield: 6 servings.

COTTAGE CHEESE SALAD

  1 (3-ounce) package lime-flavored
     gelatin
  1 (3-ounce) package lemon-flavored
     gelatin
  2 cups boiling water
1/2 cup chopped celery
1/4 cup chopped green pepper
  1 (12-ounce) carton cottage cheese
  1 (8 1/4-ounce) can crushed pineapple,
     drained
1/2 cup mayonnaise or salad dressing
  1 teaspoon minced onion

Dissolve gelatin in boiling water; chill until slightly thickened. Fold in celery, green pepper, cottage cheese, pineapple, mayonnaise or salad dressing, and onion. Pour into a 5-cup mold. Chill until firm. Yield: 8 servings.

Frozen Salads

FRUITED CHEESE SALAD

1 (3-ounce) package cream cheese, softened
1/4 cup mayonnaise
2 teaspoons lemon juice
1/8 teaspoon salt
2 tablespoons chopped maraschino cherries
1 (13 1/4-ounce) can pineapple chunks, drained
1 cup diced bananas
1/3 cup chopped walnuts
1/4 pint whipping cream, whipped

Combine cream cheese, mayonnaise, lemon juice, and salt; mix well. Add fruits and nuts. Fold whipped cream into fruit mixture. Pour into freezer tray and freeze until firm. Cut into squares and serve. Yield: 6 servings.

LIME 'N' PINE SALAD RING

2 eggs, slightly beaten
1/3 cup powdered sugar
1/4 cup lime juice
1/3 teaspoon salt
1 tablespoon butter
2 cups miniature marshmallows
1 (13 1/4-ounce) can pineapple tidbits, well drained
1 (16-ounce) can peaches, well drained and diced
1/2 pint whipping cream, whipped
Green food coloring
Cottage cheese or salad greens
Lime slices

Combine eggs, sugar, lime juice, salt, butter, and marshmallows. Cook in top of double boiler, over low heat, stirring constantly until thickened. Cool. Fold pineapple, peaches, and cooled lime mixture into whipped cream. Blend in a few drops of food coloring. Spoon into a ring mold. Freeze until firm. To serve, unmold on chilled platter and fill center of ring with cottage cheese or salad greens. Garnish with lime slices around ring. Yield: 8 servings.

FROSTY NESSELRODE MOUNTAIN

1 (8-ounce) package cream cheese, softened
1/2 cup mayonnaise
1/2 cup pineapple preserves
1/2 cup raisins
1/2 cup chopped nuts
1/2 cup halved candied cherries
1/2 pint whipping cream, whipped

Blend cream cheese with mayonnaise; add pineapple preserves, raisins, nuts, and cherries. Fold in whipped cream. Pour into pan and freeze. Serve either as salad or dessert. Yield: 4 to 6 servings.

41

APRICOT-BERRY FROST

  2 (3-ounce) packages cream cheese,
     softened
  2 tablespoons lemon juice
1/2 teaspoon salt
1/4 cup honey
  2 (17-ounce) cans apricot halves,
     drained, liquid reserved
1/4 cup apricot liquid
1/2 cup chopped pecans
1/2 pint whipping cream
1/4 cup powdered sugar
     Strawberries, raspberries, or
     blueberries for garnish

Blend cream cheese with lemon juice,
salt, honey, and apricot liquid. Add
pecans.

Whip cream, adding powdered sugar
gradually, and beat until stiff. Carefully
fold whipped cream mixture into cream
cheese mixture. Place apricot halves, cut
side down, in a 9- x 5- x 3-inch loaf pan.
Add a little cream cheese mixture and
chill. Then alternate layers of remaining
cheese mixture and fruit, reserving a few
apricot halves for garnish. Place pan in
moisture-proof bag and freeze.

To serve, unmold and place berries in
center and garnish with remaining
apricot halves. Yield: 8 servings.

FROSTED CRANBERRY CREAM SALAD

  1 (20-ounce) can crushed pineapple,
     undrained
  1 (16-ounce) can whole-berry cranberry
     sauce
  1 cup commercial sour cream
1/4 cup chopped pecans
     Salad greens

Combine pineapple, cranberry sauce,
sour cream, and pecans. Turn into an 8-
inch-square pan, cover, and freeze until
firm. Remove from freezer a few minutes
ahead of serving time. Cut into squares;
serve on salad greens. Yield: 9 servings.

FROZEN FRUIT SALAD SUPREME

  2 eggs, beaten
  2 tablespoons sugar
  2 tablespoons vinegar
 12 marshmallows, cut into pieces
1/2 pint whipping cream, whipped
  1 (30-ounce) can fruit cocktail, drained

Combine eggs, sugar, and vinegar in
top of double boiler. Cook over hot (not
boiling) water until mixture thickens.
Remove from heat and add marshmallows; stir until all are dissolved. Cool.
Fold in whipped cream and fruit cocktail.
Pour into freezer tray and freeze until
firm. Yield: 8 servings.

DELUXE FROZEN FRUIT SALAD

1/2 pint whipping cream
  2 bananas, cut into quarters
1/4 cup mayonnaise
1/4 teaspoon salt
  1 cup marshmallows
1/2 cup pecans
  2 cups diced fresh fruits

Put cream into blender and blend until
stiff. Add bananas, a few pieces at a time,
and process until bananas are well
chopped. Scrape mixture from sides of
container occasionally. Add mayonnaise
and salt. Add marshmallows, a few at a
time, and blend. Add pecans and fruits
and blend until just mixed. Pour into
freezer tray and freeze. Yield: 6 to 8
servings.

FROZEN FRUIT DELECTABLE

1/2 pint whipping cream, chilled
1/2 cup sugar
  2 tablespoons lemon juice
1/2 cup mayonnaise
  1 (17-ounce) can fruit cocktail, drained
  1 (20-ounce) can crushed pineapple, drained
1/4 cup pecans, chopped
    Parsley or maraschino cherries

Whip cream until almost stiff; beat in sugar, lemon juice, and mayonnaise. Fold in fruits and pecans. Freeze in an 8-inch-square pan. Cut into squares. Garnish with sprig of parsley or maraschino cherry. Yield: 9 servings.

PAPER CUP FROZEN SALAD

  1 (8 1/4-ounce) can crushed pineapple, drained, liquid reserved
  2 eggs, beaten
1/2 cup sugar
    Dash salt
  3 tablespoons lemon juice
  2 cups finely chopped apples
1/2 cup finely chopped celery
1/2 pint whipping cream, whipped
  6 maraschino cherries, cut in halves
12 small paper cups

Combine pineapple liquid and enough water to make 1 1/2 cups; add eggs, sugar, salt, and lemon juice; cook, stirring constantly, until thickened. Chill; fold in pineapple, apples, celery, and whipped cream. Put cherries into bottom of paper cups; pour salad into cups and freeze. Yield: 12 servings.

FROZEN FRUIT SALAD DELIGHT

  1 (3-ounce) package cream cheese, softened
1/2 cup mayonnaise
  2 tablespoons milk
  2 tablespoons lemon juice
  2 tablespoons sugar
  1 (11-ounce) can mandarin oranges, drained
  1 (16-ounce) can pitted dark sweet cherries, drained
1/2 cup chopped pecans
1/2 pint whipping cream, whipped
    Lettuce

Blend cream cheese with mayonnaise and milk; add lemon juice and sugar. Add oranges, cherries, and pecans. Fold in whipped cream.

Place 8 fluted paper muffin liners in muffin cups. Spoon salad mixture into each. Freeze until firm, at least 3 hours. To serve, peel off muffin liners and place individual salads on crisp lettuce. Serve frozen. Yield: 8 servings.

FROZEN PEACH SALAD

  3 cups peeled, crushed peaches
  2 cups miniature marshmallows
1/2 cup crushed pineapple, drained
1/2 cup slivered almonds
1/4 cup maraschino cherries, quartered
1/2 teaspoon almond extract
1/8 teaspoon salt
  2 cups commercial sour cream
    Few drops red food coloring

Combine all ingredients. Spoon into an 8-inch-square pan. Cover with foil and freeze; cut into squares and serve. Yield: 6 to 8 servings.

FROZEN SPRING SALAD

- 1 envelope (1 tablespoon) unflavored gelatin
- 1 cup cold water
- 1/3 cup sugar
- 1/2 teaspoon dry mustard
- 2 tablespoons lemon juice
- 1 cup commercial sour cream
- 2 (3-ounce) packages cream cheese, softened
- 1 (11-ounce) can mandarin oranges, drained
- 1 (16-ounce) can sliced peaches, drained
- 1 (17-ounce) can pitted dark sweet cherries, drained
- 2 cups miniature marshmallows
- 1/2 pint whipping cream, whipped
  Lettuce

Soften gelatin in cold water; place over hot water to dissolve. Combine gelatin, sugar, mustard, lemon juice, sour cream, and cream cheese; beat until well blended. Chill until mixture thickens and begins to set. Beat until smooth. Fold in fruits, marshmallows, and whipped cream. Pour into two 1-quart refrigerator trays or a 2-quart mold. Freeze. Unmold and serve on lettuce. Yield: 8 to 10 servings.

FROZEN FRUIT SALAD

- 2 (3-ounce) packages cream cheese, softened
- 3/4 cup salad dressing (not mayonnaise)
- 1 (17-ounce) can fruit cocktail, undrained
- 1 (13 1/4-ounce) can crushed pineapple, undrained

Combine cream cheese and salad dressing and mix to blend. Stir in fruits and mix well. Put into individual molds, seal securely, and freeze. Unmold and serve before fruits have thawed completely. Yield: 6 to 8 servings.

FROSTY FRUIT SALAD

- 2 (3-ounce) packages cream cheese, softened
- 1/3 cup mayonnaise or salad dressing
- 2 tablespoons lemon juice
- 1/4 cup sugar
- 1 teaspoon salt
- 1 1/2 cups miniature marshmallows
- 1 (13 1/4-ounce) can pineapple chunks, well drained
- 1/2 cup chopped walnuts
- 1 medium-size orange, peeled and cubed
- 1/4 cup red maraschino cherries, halved
- 1/4 cup green maraschino cherries, halved
- 1/2 pint whipping cream, whipped
  Salad greens

Combine cream cheese, mayonnaise or salad dressing, lemon juice, sugar, and salt. Beat with rotary beater until well blended. Stir in rest of ingredients except whipped cream; then gently fold in cream. Spoon mixture into 2 freezer trays and freeze overnight. To serve, let stand at room temperature several minutes; slice and serve on crisp salad greens. Yield: 10 or 12 servings.

FROZEN CHRISTMAS SALAD

    4 (3-ounce) packages cream cheese,
      softened
    1 (16-ounce) can cranberry sauce
 1/2 cup mayonnaise
    2 cups chopped pecans
    1 (4-ounce) bottle chopped maraschino
      cherries, undrained
    1 (8 1/4-ounce) can crushed pineapple,
      drained
   12 graham crackers or 15 to 18 vanilla
      wafers, crushed
      Lettuce

Beat cream cheese in a large bowl. Add
cranberry sauce and mayonnaise and mix
well. Add pecans, cherries, pineapple,
and graham cracker or vanilla wafer
crumbs. Spoon into an 8-inch-square pan
and cover with foil. Freeze until ready to
serve. Cut into squares and serve on
lettuce leaves. Yield: 6 servings.

PINK ARCTIC FREEZE

    2 (3-ounce) packages cream cheese,
      softened
    2 tablespoons sugar
    2 tablespoons mayonnaise
    1 (16-ounce) can jellied cranberry sauce
    1 cup drained, crushed pineapple
 1/2 cup chopped pecans
 1/4 pint whipping cream, whipped
      Lettuce

Cream together cheese and sugar; stir
in mayonnaise. Fold in cranberry sauce,
pineapple, pecans, and whipped cream.
Spoon into a 9- x 5- x 3-inch loaf pan.
Freeze until firm. Cut into slices and serve
on lettuce. (May also be frozen in round
cans, unmolded, and served in slices.)
Yield: 8 servings.

FROZEN CRANBERRY SALAD

    2 (3-ounce) packages cream cheese,
      softened and whipped
    2 tablespoons mayonnaise
    2 tablespoons sugar
    1 (8 1/4-ounce) can crushed pineapple,
      undrained
    1 (16-ounce) can whole cranberries
 1/2 cup chopped nuts
 1/2 pint whipping cream, whipped

Combine cream cheese, mayonnaise,
sugar, and pineapple, then cranberries
and nuts. Fold in whipped cream. Put into
individual molds. Freeze. Yield: 8 to 10
servings.

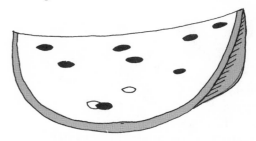

FROZEN DATE SALAD

    1 (8-ounce) package cream cheese,
      softened
    1 (8 1/4-ounce) can crushed pineapple,
      undrained
    1 cup chopped, pitted dates
    8 maraschino cherries, chopped
    1 tablespoon lemon juice
 1/8 teaspoon salt
 1/2 pint whipping cream, whipped, or
      packaged whipped topping
    2 tablespoons chopped nuts

Blend cream cheese and pineapple. Add
dates, cherries, lemon juice, and salt. Fold
in whipped cream or whipped topping
and nuts. Pour into a 1-quart mold or
individual molds. Freeze until firm.
Unmold. Yield: 8 servings.

Garnishes

Garnishes dress up the appearance of all kinds of food, adding eye appeal and stimulating the appetite. Garnishes should be simple and natural and not overdone. Fresh fruits and vegetables make attractive accents and provide flavor and texture contrast. You'll find these decorative garnishes surprisingly easy to make.

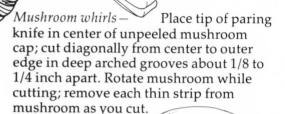

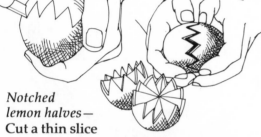

Notched lemon halves—
Cut a thin slice from each end of lemon to make flat bases. Make a small cut slanting downward into center of lemon with blade of small, sharp knife. Remove blade. Make a small cut slanting upward, forming a zigzag. Continue slanting cuts in zigzag pattern all around lemon. Separate halves by gently pulling apart.

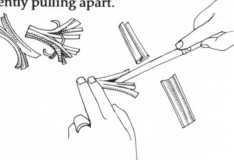

Celery curls— Cut stalks into 2-inch pieces. Cut several slits at each end of celery, cutting almost to center. Place in ice water for ends to curl.

Mushroom whirls— Place tip of paring knife in center of unpeeled mushroom cap; cut diagonally from center to outer edge in deep arched grooves about 1/8 to 1/4 inch apart. Rotate mushroom while cutting; remove each thin strip from mushroom as you cut.

Radish roses—
Trim ends of large radishes. Beginning at stem end and continuing around radish, make horizontal slits about 1/4 inch deep, slanting sharp knife downward. To make petals, slice small radish into very thin slices and insert in slits. Place in ice water to open. For an easier version, cut slits deeper to form the petals.

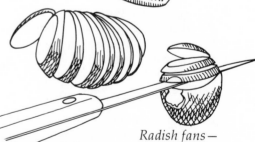

Radish fans—
Select long radishes; trim both ends. With sharp knife, cut radishes crosswise into very thin slices, cutting only 3/4s of the way through. Place radishes in ice water; refrigerate several hours for radishes to open. Drain well before using.

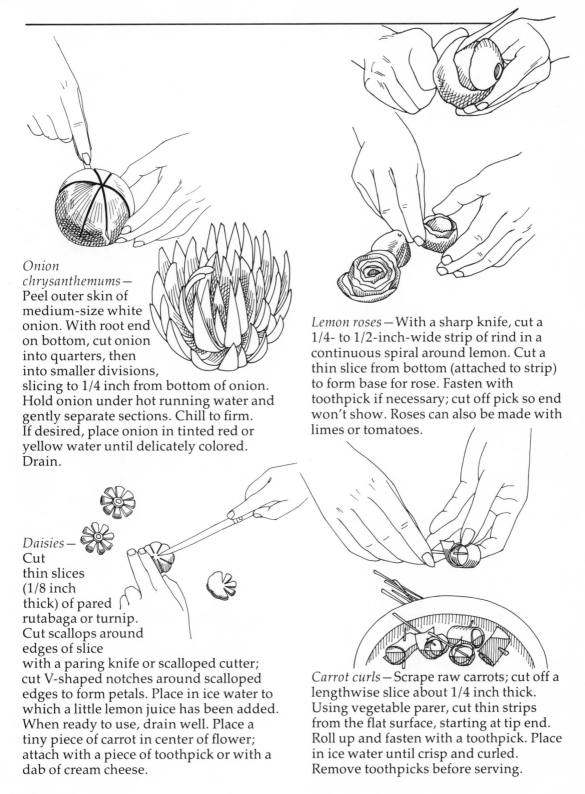

Onion chrysanthemums— Peel outer skin of medium-size white onion. With root end on bottom, cut onion into quarters, then into smaller divisions, slicing to 1/4 inch from bottom of onion. Hold onion under hot running water and gently separate sections. Chill to firm. If desired, place onion in tinted red or yellow water until delicately colored. Drain.

Lemon roses— With a sharp knife, cut a 1/4- to 1/2-inch-wide strip of rind in a continuous spiral around lemon. Cut a thin slice from bottom (attached to strip) to form base for rose. Fasten with toothpick if necessary; cut off pick so end won't show. Roses can also be made with limes or tomatoes.

Daisies— Cut thin slices (1/8 inch thick) of pared rutabaga or turnip. Cut scallops around edges of slice with a paring knife or scalloped cutter; cut V-shaped notches around scalloped edges to form petals. Place in ice water to which a little lemon juice has been added. When ready to use, drain well. Place a tiny piece of carrot in center of flower; attach with a piece of toothpick or with a dab of cream cheese.

Carrot curls— Scrape raw carrots; cut off a lengthwise slice about 1/4 inch thick. Using vegetable parer, cut thin strips from the flat surface, starting at tip end. Roll up and fasten with a toothpick. Place in ice water until crisp and curled. Remove toothpicks before serving.

Salad Greens

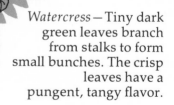

French or Belgian Endive —
Creamy white leaves grow in a tightly folded elongated head. The small leaves are slightly bitter.

Know your salad greens so you can put color, flavor, texture, and interest into your salads. For both taste and eye appeal, a combination of several greens makes an interesting salad.

- Fresh, crisp greens are essential for success in salad making, so select the best quality available.
- Remove any wilted leaves; wash greens well in tepid water. Handle greens gently as they bruise easily.
- Drain greens after washing; pat dry with paper towels.
- Store cleaned greens in refrigerator in a crisper or plastic bag.
- When preparing salad, tear, rather than cut, greens into bite-size pieces.

Iceberg — The most popular lettuce. A firm, crisp-textured head having green leaves on the outside with a pale green core. Curly leaves overlap slightly but can be separated into cups for various salads.

Green Cabbage —
A firm head with tightly crimped and heavily veined green leaves. Leaves vary from bright green to silvery green.

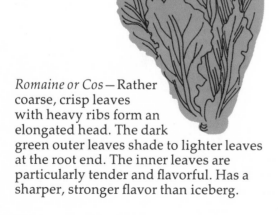

Romaine or Cos — Rather coarse, crisp leaves with heavy ribs form an elongated head. The dark green outer leaves shade to lighter leaves at the root end. The inner leaves are particularly tender and flavorful. Has a sharper, stronger flavor than iceberg.

Watercress — Tiny dark green leaves branch from stalks to form small bunches. The crisp leaves have a pungent, tangy flavor.

Boston or Butterhead — A head slightly softly, lighter, and less crisp than iceberg. Outer leaves are dark green and inner ones are light yellow. Velvety leaves have a delicate flavor and are easily separated.

Chinese or Celery Cabbage — A firm, tapering stalk (about 14 to 16 inches long) forms a compact head that looks like romaine and has characteristics similar to romaine and cabbage. The tightly closed broad leaves are crisp; the color is pale green to white.

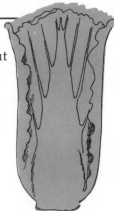

Escarole — Broad, flat leaves with ruffly edges shade from rich green outer leaves to yellowish center leaves. Has a mild to slightly bitter flavor.

Leaf — Pale green, delicate leaves grow loosely from a small, slender stalk. Ruffled leaves are crisp in texture and sweet in flavor.

Chicory or Curly Endive — A large, bunchy head of tightly curled and lacy dark green outer leaves with yellowish white leaves at core. Center leaves are milder in flavor than the slightly bitter outer leaves.

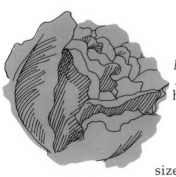

Bibb or Limestone — A tiny cup-shaped head of deep green leaves, becoming whitish green toward the core. Prized for its size, color, and flavor.

Spinach — Dark green, slightly curly leaves with coarse stems grow on stocky plants which have a number of branches. Remove stems and use young, tender leaves for salads.

Green Salads

Combine all ingredients and mix well. Serve over salad greens. Yield: 1 cup.

GREEN AND GOLD SALAD

1/2 cup olive oil
2 tablespoons red wine vinegar
2 tablespoons lemon juice, divided
1 clove garlic, halved
1 tablespoon chopped parsley
1 teaspoon salt
1 teaspoon dry mustard
  Freshly ground black pepper
2 avocados
6 cups lettuce, torn into bite-size pieces
4 cups spinach, well washed and torn into bite-size pieces
1 cup sliced stuffed olives
2 large oranges, peeled and sectioned
1/2 red onion, thinly sliced

Combine oil, vinegar, 1 tablespoon lemon juice, garlic, parsley, salt, mustard, and pepper; chill. At serving time, peel and slice avocados; brush with remaining 1 tablespoon lemon juice. Arrange with remaining ingredients in salad bowl and toss with dressing. Serve at once. Yield: 8 servings.

FRESH SPINACH-MUSHROOM SALAD

1 pound fresh spinach, well washed and torn into bite-size pieces
1/2 pound fresh mushrooms, washed, halved, and sliced
  Grated rind of 1 lemon
1/4 cup salad oil
  Juice of 1 large lemon

Combine spinach and mushrooms in a large bowl. Combine grated lemon rind, salad oil, and lemon juice. Just before serving, pour over spinach-mushroom mixture and toss gently to coat. Yield: 8 servings.

ESQUIRE SALAD

2 heads Bibb lettuce, washed
4 green onions, sliced
6 fresh mushrooms, sliced
4 cherry tomatoes, sliced
2 artichoke hearts, cut into quarters
  Dressing

Prepare salad ingredients in large bowl. Add dressing and toss lightly. Yield: 2 servings.

Dressing:

3/4 cup olive oil
1/4 cup wine vinegar
  Juice of 1/2 lemon
  Dash Worcestershire sauce
  Salt and pepper to taste
  Dash tarragon
  Dash chopped parsley
  Dash oregano
  Dash basil
  Dash garlic powder

LOUIS PAPPAS'S FAMOUS GREEK SALAD

  6 boiling potatoes, unpeeled
  2 medium-size onions or 4 green
    onions, sliced
1/2 cup thinly sliced green pepper
1/4 cup finely chopped parsley
    Salt to taste
1/2 cup salad dressing or mayonnaise
  1 large head lettuce
 12 roka leaves or 12 sprigs watercress
  2 tomatoes, cut into 6 wedges each
  1 cucumber, peeled and cut lengthwise
    into 8 fingers
  1 avocado, peeled and cut into wedges
  4 portions of feta (Greek cheese)
  1 green pepper, cut into 8 rings
  4 slices canned beets
  4 shrimp, cooked and peeled
  4 anchovy filets
 12 black olives (Greek style preferred)
 12 medium-hot Salonika peppers
  4 fancy-cut radishes
  4 whole green onions
1/2 cup distilled white vinegar
1/4 cup each olive and salad oil, blended
    Oregano to taste

Boil the potatoes for about 30 minutes or until tender but not soft; drain, cool, and peel, and slice into a bowl. Add onion, green pepper, and parsley; sprinkle lightly with salt. Fold in salad dressing or mayonnaise, using more if necessary to hold salad together lightly.

Line a large platter with outside lettuce leaves and place 3 cups of potato salad in a mound in the center of the platter. Cover with remaining lettuce, which has been shredded. Arrange roka or watercress on top of this. Place tomato wedges around the outer edges of the salad, with a few on top. Add cucumber fingers in between the tomatoes, making a solid base of the salad. Place avocado wedges around the outside of the mound.

Arrange slices of feta on top of the salad, with green pepper rings over all. On the very top, place the beets with a shrimp on each beet and an anchovy filet on the shrimp. The olives, peppers, radishes, and green onions may be arranged as desired. Sprinkle vinegar over the top; then sprinkle with the blended oils. Sprinkle oregano over all, and serve at once. Yield: 4 servings.

CAPTAIN'S SALAD

  1 quart leaf lettuce or romaine, torn
    into bite-size pieces
  1 quart spinach leaves, torn into bite-
    size pieces
1/2 cup small sweet onion rings
  3 tablespoons toasted sesame seeds
  1 teaspoon salt
1/4 teaspoon pepper
1/2 teaspoon dry mustard
  3 tablespoons vinegar
  1 tablespoon honey
1/2 cup salad oil
  3 tomatoes, peeled and cut into wedges
  2 cups herb-seasoned croutons

Combine greens, onion rings, and sesame seeds; toss and refrigerate until just before serving.

Make salad dressing by combining salt, pepper, and mustard in small mixing bowl; stir in vinegar and honey. Slowly add salad oil while beating with rotary beater or electric mixer; refrigerate.

Just before serving, combine greens, salad dressing, tomato wedges, and croutons; toss. Serve immediately from chilled salad bowl. Yield: 8 to 10 servings.

WESTERN SALAD BOWL

    1/4 cup salad oil or olive oil
      2 cloves garlic, finely chopped
      1 tablespoon Worcestershire sauce
    1/4 teaspoon pepper
    1/2 cup grated Parmesan cheese
    1/4 cup crumbled blue cheese
      1 egg
  3 1/2 tablespoons lemon juice
      2 quarts mixed salad greens
      2 cups small bread cubes, toasted

Combine oil and garlic; let stand at room temperature for several hours. Combine Worcestershire, pepper, salt, cheeses, egg, and lemon juice; blend well and toss with salad greens. Strain garlic from oil; discard. Toss oil with toasted bread cubes. Add to salad and toss again. Yield: 8 to 10 servings.

WILTED ENDIVE SALAD

      1 large head endive, washed and
         separated
      5 slices bacon, fried, drained and
         crumbled, drippings reserved
      1 onion, thinly sliced
    1/4 cup bacon drippings
    1/2 cup sugar (less if desired)
      1 teaspoon salt
    1/4 cup vinegar
         Water, if needed to thin (optional)

Toss endive with bacon and onion slices. Combine bacon drippings, sugar, salt, vinegar, and water, if desired; heat until mixture bubbles and sugar dissolves. Pour hot dressing over salad greens. Toss thoroughly so greens are wilted. Serve immediately. Yield: 6 servings.

TOSSED SPINACH-ORANGE SALAD

      3 cups fresh spinach, well washed and
         torn into small pieces
      3 medium-size oranges, sectioned
      1 tablespoon sugar
         Salt to taste
    1/4 cup French Dressing

Combine spinach, orange sections, sugar, and salt in a large bowl. Add 1/4 cup (or more, if desired) French Dressing and toss. Yield: 6 to 8 servings.

French Dressing:

      1 teaspoon salt
    1/4 teaspoon sugar
      3 tablespoons lemon juice
    1/4 cup catsup
    1/2 cup salad oil
      1 (3-ounce) package cream cheese,
         softened (optional)

Combine the first 5 ingredients in a pint jar; shake well and let sit several hours before using. Cream cheese may be added to the dressing just before serving, if desired. Yield: 1 cup.

TOSSED LETTUCE AND MUSHROOM SALAD

      1 medium-size head lettuce
    1/2 small bunch watercress, torn into
         bite-size pieces
    1/4 pound (1 cup) very small whole white
         mushroom caps
         Commercial French dressing

Wash lettuce and watercress; pat dry and tear into bite-size pieces. Place in a salad bowl. Wash mushrooms and add along with French dressing. Toss lightly, but thoroughly, to coat each piece of lettuce and watercress. Serve at once. Yield: 6 servings.

TASTY GREEN SALAD

1 small head lettuce, torn into bite-size pieces
1 (17-ounce) can green peas, drained
1 medium-size onion, chopped
1 cup favorite salad dressing
1 cup shredded Swiss cheese
1/2 cup bacon bits

Layer all ingredients in a bowl in the order given. Marinate in crisper unit of refrigerator or in a tightly covered bowl at least 10 hours. Yield: 10 servings.

WILTED LETTUCE SALAD

4 cups lettuce, torn into bite-size pieces
3 green onions with tops, chopped
5 slices bacon, fried, drained and crumbled, drippings reserved
1/2 to 1 teaspoon salt
1 teaspoon sugar
2 tablespoons vinegar

Put lettuce in a large bowl, add onion, and toss mixture lightly. Combine hot bacon drippings, salt, sugar, and vinegar. Stir well, heat, and pour immediately over lettuce; toss lightly to coat all leaves. Sprinkle bacon over top. Yield: 3 to 4 servings.

HEALTHFUL ICEBERG LETTUCE

Juice of 1/2 lemon, strained
1 tomato, peeled, diced, and sieved
1/2 small onion, minced
1 clove garlic, minced
1 ripe avocado, peeled and mashed
1 teaspoon salt
Dash cayenne pepper
1 tablespoon salad oil
1 1/2 heads iceberg lettuce, cut into 6 wedges and chilled

Combine lemon juice, tomato, onion, garlic, and avocado. Stir in salt, cayenne pepper, and salad oil; blend well.

Arrange iceberg lettuce wedges on platter and pass dressing. Yield: 6 servings.

HEAD LETTUCE AND ANCHOVY SALAD

1 clove garlic
1 head lettuce, broken into chunks
1 (2-ounce) can anchovy filets, cut into pieces
4 hard-cooked eggs, sliced
1/8 teaspoon freshly ground black pepper
2 tablespoons salad oil
2 tablespoons lemon juice

Rub salad bowl with clove of garlic. Combine ingredients. Toss lightly. Yield: 6 servings.

SWISS YODEL SALAD

1 small head crisp lettuce, torn into bite-size pieces
1 bunch watercress, sprigs snipped in half
1/2 pound Swiss cheese, cut into thin strips
1/4 cup mayonnaise
1 tablespoon prepared mustard
1/2 teaspoon paprika
2 tablespoons salad oil
1 tablespoon wine vinegar
Red onion rings (optional)

Wash greens; pat dry. Mix greens and cheese. Combine mayonnaise, mustard, paprika, salad oil, and vinegar. Pour over salad and toss. Serve with chilled red onion rings, if desired. Yield: 6 servings.

Meat, Poultry, and Seafood Salads

Combine beef, onion, and green pepper; add salad dressing or mayonnaise and mix well. Place mixture in lettuce-lined bowl; garnish with tomato wedges and egg quarters. Top salad with anchovy filets. Yield: 6 servings.

CORN BEEF SALAD

      1 envelope (1 tablespoon) unflavored gelatin
      2 tablespoons cold water
      1 (10 1/2-ounce) can beef consommé
      1 (12-ounce) can corn beef, broken into bite-size pieces
      1 cup chopped celery
    3/4 cup mayonnaise
    1/4 cup salad dressing
         Salad greens

Soften gelatin in cold water. Heat consommé, add gelatin, and stir until dissolved. Set aside to cool. Combine corn beef, celery, mayonnaise, and salad dressing; mix well. Add cooled consommé and mix well to blend. Chill. Serve on salad greens. Yield: 6 servings.

VEAL AND HAM SALAD

      3 tablespoons mayonnaise
    1/3 cup commercial sour cream
    1/4 teaspoon salt
    1/8 teaspoon pepper
      1 tablespoon capers
      2 cups cooked, julienned, veal
  1 1/2 cups cooked, julienned, ham
    2/3 cup thinly sliced cucumber
    1/2 cup diced celery
         Lettuce

Combine mayonnaise, sour cream, salt, pepper, and capers; toss lightly with veal, ham, cucumber, and celery. Serve on lettuce. Yield: 6 servings.

BEEF SALAD BOWL

  1 1/2 pounds boiled beef, sliced
      1 cup thinly sliced onion
      1 green pepper, julienned
      1 cup salad dressing or mayonnaise
         Lettuce leaves
      3 tomatoes, cut into wedges
      3 hard-cooked eggs, cut into quarters
     12 anchovy filets

SKILLET HAM-POTATO SALAD

1/4 cup chopped green onion
1/4 cup chopped green pepper
 1 (12-ounce) can chopped ham,
   separated
 1 tablespoon butter or margarine
 3 cups cooked, pared, and cubed
   potatoes
1/4 teaspoon salt
   Dash pepper
1/4 cup mayonnaise or salad dressing
1/2 pound sharp pasteurized process
   American cheese, diced
 2 tablespoons chopped parsley

Cook onion, green pepper, and ham in hot butter or margarine, stirring occasionally, until meat is lightly browned. Add potatoes, salt, pepper, and mayonnaise or salad dressing. Heat, mixing lightly. Stir in cheese, and heat just until cheese begins to melt. Sprinkle with parsley. Yield: 4 servings.

SALMAGUNDI

 3 quarts salad greens (Boston, romaine,
   endive, and watercress)
 1 pound cooked ham, julienned
 1 pound chicken or turkey, julienned
 4 hard-cooked eggs, sliced
16 sweet gherkins
 8 celery hearts
16 sardines
16 anchovy filets
   Oil and Vinegar Dressing

Arrange salad greens on individual salad plates or on a large platter. Place ham, chicken, eggs, gherkins, celery, sardines, and anchovies in a pattern over and around the salad greens. Sprinkle lightly with Oil and Vinegar Dressing. Yield: 8 servings.

Oil and Vinegar Dressing:

 1 teaspoon salt
3/4 teaspoon white pepper
1/2 cup cider vinegar
1/2 cup salad oil

Combine all ingredients in a jar; cover tightly. Before serving, shake well to blend. Yield: 1 cup.

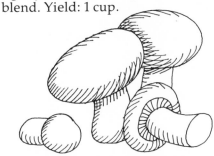

HOT POTATO SALAD WITH FRANKFURTERS

 8 cups cooked, peeled, and diced
   potatoes
 2 teaspoons salt
1/8 teaspoon pepper
1/4 cup vinegar
1/4 cup salad oil
1/2 cup chopped onion
 1 cup chopped celery
1/4 cup diced pimiento
 8 frankfurters
   Few sprigs parsley
 5 strips pimiento

Sprinkle potatoes with salt and pepper; pour vinegar and salad oil over potatoes and let stand until all the vinegar and oil is absorbed. Add onion, celery, and the diced pimiento.
Cut frankfurters into 1-inch pieces; add to potatoes. Place salad in a 2 1/2-quart baking dish. Cover and bake at 350° for 40 minutes. Remove cover and continue baking for 10 minutes. Garnish with parsley and the pimiento strips. Yield: 8 servings.

MEXICAN SALAD

4 cups shredded lettuce
1/2 cup sliced green onion
1 pound ground beef, browned
1/4 cup chopped onion
1 (15-ounce) can ranch-style beans,
   drained
1/2 cup commercial French dressing
1/2 cup water
1 tablespoon chili powder
1 (8-ounce) wedge Cheddar cheese,
   shredded and divided
   Tortilla chips

Combine lettuce and green onion in
large salad bowl; let stand. Into skillet
with browned beef, add onion and cook
until tender. Stir in beans, French
dressing, water, and chili powder;
simmer 15 minutes.

Add meat mixture and 1 1/2 cups
cheese to lettuce and green onion. Toss
lightly. Sprinkle with remaining cheese
and serve immediately with tortilla chips.
Yield: 6 to 8 servings.

FRANKFURTER SALAD

8 frankfurters, cooked and sliced
2 cups cooked, diced potatoes
2/3 cup chopped onion
1/4 cup chopped green pepper
1/2 cup chopped cucumber
1 tablespoon prepared mustard
1/3 cup chili sauce
2/3 cup salad dressing or mayonnaise

Combine frankfurters and vegetables.
Combine mustard, chili sauce, and salad
dressing or mayonnaise; add to
frankfurter mixture. Toss lightly. Yield: 6
servings.

HEARTY SUPPER SALAD

1/2 pound frankfurters, thinly sliced
1 tablespoon corn oil
1 green pepper, cut into narrow strips
1/2 cup thinly sliced celery
2 potatoes, cooked and diced
1/2 cup finely chopped onion
1/2 cup commercial French dressing
1 teaspoon salt
1/4 teaspoon pepper
1 head lettuce, shredded
1/4 cup Swiss cheese, cut into thin strips
2 tomatoes, cut into thin wedges

Sauté frankfurters in corn oil until
lightly browned. Remove from skillet and
combine with green pepper, celery,
potatoes, onion, French dressing, salt, and
pepper. Cover and chill. Just before
serving, add lettuce, cheese, and tomato
wedges. Toss gently to mix. Yield: 8 to 10
servings.

SKILLET HAM SALAD

1/4 cup chopped green onion
1/4 cup chopped green pepper
2 cups cooked, diced ham
1 tablespoon salad oil
3 or 4 medium-size potatoes, cooked
   and diced
1/4 teaspoon salt
   Dash pepper
1/4 cup mayonnaise or salad dressing
1 1/2 cups diced sharp pasteurized
   process American cheese

Cook onion, green pepper, and ham in
hot oil, stirring occasionally, until ham is
lightly browned. Add potatoes, salt,
pepper, and mayonnaise or salad
dressing. Heat, mixing lightly. Stir in
cheese; heat just until cheese begins to
melt. Yield: 4 servings.

APPLE AND HAM SALAD

  2 cups unpeeled diced apples
  2 cups cooked, diced ham
1/2 cup diced celery
1/4 teaspoon salt
  2 tablespoons lemon juice
1/8 teaspoon pepper
     Dash garlic powder
1/4 cup mayonnaise
     Lettuce
     Parsley

   Combine all ingredients except lettuce
and parsley; toss lightly. Serve on lettuce
and garnish with parsley. Yield: 4 to 5
servings.

HAM AND MACARONI SALAD

  2 cups uncooked elbow macaroni
  1 (1 3/4-ounce) envelope chili mix
  1 cup mayonnaise
1/2 cup sweet pickle relish
  2 cups diced celery
  2 to 3 cups cooked, diced ham
  2 tomatoes, cut into wedges

   Cook macaroni according to package
directions; drain well. Sprinkle chili mix
directly from package onto macaroni.
Blend in mayonnaise and pickle relish;
chill. Add celery and ham; toss to mix.
Garnish with tomato wedges. Yield: 8
servings.

HUNGARIAN TONGUE SALAD

  3 cups cooked, diced tongue
  1 cup grated carrot
1/2 cup finely chopped celery
1/4 cup finely chopped green pepper
1/4 teaspoon paprika
3/4 cup commercial French dressing
     Lettuce
     Parsley, chopped
     Mayonnaise

   Combine tongue, carrot, celery, and
green pepper. Combine paprika and
French dressing; add to tongue mixture.
Chill and marinate at least 1 to 2 hours.
Drain. Serve on lettuce. Garnish with
parsley; top with mayonnaise. Yield: 5 to
6 servings.

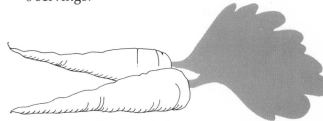

MEATY MAIN-DISH SALAD

  1 (12-ounce) can luncheon meat, cut
     into 1/4-inch cubes
1/4 cup commercial garlic-oil salad
     dressing
  1 cup diced celery
  1 tablespoon sweet pickle relish
  2 hard-cooked eggs, chopped
1/4 cup mayonnaise
     Salt and pepper to taste
  6 medium-size tomatoes
     Lettuce cups

   Marinate and chill meat cubes in garlic
dressing 2 to 4 hours; drain. Add celery,
relish, eggs, mayonnaise, salt, and
pepper. Cutting to within 1/2 inch of
bottom, cut each tomato into sixths and
spread apart. Fill center with meat salad.
Serve on lettuce cups. Yield: 6 servings.

CELESTIAL CHICKEN SALAD

    4 cups cooked, diced chicken
    2 cups diced celery
    1 (4 1/2-ounce) jar whole mushrooms, drained
1/2 cup pecan halves, toasted
    4 slices bacon, fried and crumbled
    1 cup mayonnaise or salad dressing
    1 cup commercial sour cream
1 1/2 teaspoons salt
    2 tablespoons lemon juice
      Lettuce cups (optional)

Combine chicken, celery, mushrooms, pecans, and bacon in a large bowl. Blend mayonnaise or salad dressing with remaining ingredients. Add to chicken mixture, tossing lightly to mix. Chill thoroughly. Serve in crisp lettuce cups, if desired. Yield: 6 to 8 servings.

CHICKEN IN ASPIC

    2 envelopes (2 tablespoons) unflavored gelatin
    2 cups cold water, divided
    2 (10 1/2-ounce) cans consommé
1/2 teaspoon salt
    4 tablespoons lemon juice
    2 cups cooked, diced chicken
    1 cup mixed cooked vegetables
1/2 cup chopped celery
    4 tablespoons chopped green pepper
    4 tablespoons chopped pimiento

Sprinkle gelatin on 1 cup cold water; let sit until gelatin has softened. Place over low heat and cook, stirring constantly, until gelatin is dissolved. Remove from heat; add remaining cold water, consommé, salt, and lemon juice. Chill until mixture is consistency of unbeaten egg white. Fold in remaining ingredients. Spoon into a 6-cup mold or individual molds. Chill until firm. Yield: 8 servings.

CHICKEN-APRICOT SALAD

1/2 cup mayonnaise
    1 cup commercial sour cream
1/4 cup milk
    2 tablespoons lemon juice
    2 teaspoons prepared mustard
    1 teaspoon salt
    1 cup dried apricots, diced
    3 cups cooked, diced chicken
    1 cup chopped celery
1/3 cup finely chopped scallions
      Lettuce

Blend mayonnaise, sour cream, milk, lemon juice, mustard, and salt in large bowl; add apricots, chicken, celery, and scallions. Toss lightly until combined; chill. Spoon salad into lettuce-lined bowl. Yield: 6 servings.

SUMMER BREEZE CHICKEN SALAD

    2 (5-ounce) cans chicken, drained and diced
    1 (6-ounce) can water chestnuts, drained and chopped
    2 tablespoons chopped walnuts
1/4 cup chopped green pepper
1/4 teaspoon salt
1/3 cup commercial French dressing
      Sliced cucumbers
      Tomatoes, sliced 1/2 inch thick

Combine chicken, water chestnuts, walnuts, green pepper, salt, and French dressing. Mix well. To serve, place a cucumber slice on a tomato slice and top with a scoop of chicken salad. Yield: 4 to 6 servings.

CHICKEN LIVER SALAD

  1 **pound broiler-fryer chicken livers**
  1 **teaspoon Ac'cent**
  1 **teaspoon salt**
  1 **teaspoon pepper**
1/4 **cup corn oil**
  1 **teaspoon crushed rosemary**
1/2 **cup chopped pimiento**
  1 **tablespoon chopped onion**
  2 **hard-cooked eggs, chopped**
  1 **tablespoon chopped celery**
     About 1/2 cup mayonnaise

Blot chicken livers dry. Sprinkle with Ac'cent, salt, and pepper. Heat corn oil in an 11-inch skillet over medium heat. Add livers and cook slowly for about 20 minutes. Set aside; chop. Mix rosemary, pimiento, onion, eggs, celery, and mayonnaise. (Use more or less mayonnaise, depending on way served.) Mix and blend in chopped liver. This mixture can be used as a dip, sandwich filling, or salad served on lettuce. Yield: 3 cups.

DIETERS' DINNER SALAD

1 **head iceberg lettuce, torn into bite-size chunks, rinsed, and drained**
1 **red apple, cored, quartered, and thinly sliced**
   Lemon juice (optional)
1 **(16-ounce) can cut green beans, drained**
2 **cups cooked, cubed chicken**

Chill lettuce in plastic bag or plastic crisper.
Place lettuce on serving platter or in individual salad bowls. Sprinkle apple with lemon juice, if desired. Arrange apple, beans, and chicken on lettuce. Serve with Dieters' Dressing. Yield: 6 servings.

Dieters' Dressing:

  1 **teaspoon grated lemon rind**
1/3 **cup lemon juice**
1/4 **cup corn oil**
  1 **tablespoon honey**
  1 **teaspoon salt**
1/2 **teaspoon celery seeds**
1/4 **teaspoon garlic powder**
  3 **dashes hot sauce**

Combine all ingredients; pour into a jar with cover; chill.

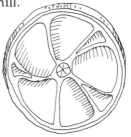

CONGEALED CHICKEN SALAD

  2 **envelopes (2 tablespoons) unflavored gelatin**
1/2 **cup cold water**
  1 **cup mayonnaise**
  2 **cups cooked, chopped chicken**
  1 **teaspoon salt**
1/2 **cup diced celery**
1/4 **cup chopped stuffed olives**
  3 **tablespoons chopped pimiento**
  2 **tablespoons finely chopped onion**
  3 **tablespoons lemon juice**
1 1/2 **teaspoons prepared horseradish**
  2 **tablespoons diced green pepper**
1/4 **teaspoon paprika**
  1 **cup chopped almonds**
1/2 **pint whipping cream, whipped**

Soften gelatin in cold water; dissolve over hot water. Cool slightly and stir into mayonnaise. Add all other ingredients except the whipped cream and mix well. Fold whipped cream into mixture. Put into oiled loaf pan and chill until firm. Yield: 8 to 10 servings.

CHICKEN RAMBLER SALAD

   Salad greens, torn into pieces
1 medium-size onion, chopped
1 (16-ounce) can or jar sliced pickled
   beets, drained
1 (16-ounce) can peas, drained
1 (5-ounce) can boned chicken or turkey,
   cut into bite-size pieces
2 hard-cooked eggs, sliced
   Commercial French dressing or
   mayonnaise

   Combine salad greens and onion and
place in serving dish. Arrange beets, peas,
chicken or turkey, and eggs on the greens.
Serve with French dressing or
mayonnaise. Yield: 6 servings.

WILD RICE AND TURKEY SALAD

1/2 pound wild rice, cooked and cooled
   4 cups cooked, chopped turkey or
      chicken
   1 cup mayonnaise
1/2 cup commercial French dressing
      Salt to taste
   1 (5-ounce) can sliced almonds
   1 cup diced celery
   2 (11-ounce) cans mandarin oranges,
      drained
   1 (20-ounce) can pineapple tidbits,
      drained
      Lettuce

   Combine rice, turkey or chicken,
mayonnaise, French dressing, salt,
almonds, and celery. Chill. Just before
serving, add oranges and pineapple.
Serve on lettuce. Yield: 8 to 10 servings.

MOLDED CHICKEN SALAD

2 envelopes (2 tablespoons) unflavored
   gelatin
1/2 cup cold water
3/4 cup mayonnaise or salad dressing
      Salt, pepper, paprika, and vinegar to
      taste
   1 to 1 1/2 cups cooked, diced chicken
   1 cup finely chopped celery
1/2 cup chopped olives
1/2 cup cooked, diced chestnuts
   3 tablespoons chopped pimiento
      Several sprigs chopped parsley
      Lettuce

   Soften gelatin in cold water; dissolve
over hot water and stir until completely
dissolved. Cool slightly, then fold in
mayonnaise or salad dressing, salt,
pepper, paprika, and vinegar to taste.
Add other ingredients except lettuce and
mix well. Turn into an oiled mold and
chill until congealed. Unmold on bed of
lettuce or other greens. Yield: 6 servings.

HOT CHICKEN OR SEAFOOD SALAD

2 cups cooked, diced chicken (or crab
   or shrimp)
1 cup thinly sliced celery
1/2 cup cashews
1/2 teaspoon salt
1 onion, grated
1 cup mayonnaise
2 tablespoons lemon juice
1/2 cup shredded Cheddar cheese
1 cup crushed potato chips

   Combine all ingredients except cheese
and potato chips. Pile lightly in casserole
or individual baking dishes. Sprinkle
with cheese and potato chips. Bake at 400°
about 20 minutes or until mixture is
heated and cheese is melted. Yield: 6
servings.

JELLIED CHICKEN SALAD

2 envelopes (2 tablespoons) unflavored gelatin
1/2 cup cold water
2 cups boiling water
1 teaspoon fresh chopped dill or 1/2 teaspoon dillweed
1 teaspoon salt
1 tablespoon sugar
1 to 2 tablespoons wine vinegar
2 tablespoons lemon juice
1 tablespoon grated onion
6 to 8 thin cucumber slices
2 (4 3/4-ounce) cans chicken spread
1 cup finely chopped celery
2 tablespoons chopped pimiento
1 cup commercial sour cream
Salt and pepper to taste

Soften gelatin in cold water; dissolve in boiling water. Combine half of gelatin mixture with dill, salt, sugar, vinegar, lemon juice, and onion; chill until slightly thickened. Line edge of 1-quart mold with cucumber slices; carefully pour in the chilled gelatin. Chill until firm.

Combine chicken spread, celery, pimiento, and sour cream with remaining gelatin mixture; season with salt and pepper. Chill until slightly thickened; then spoon over firm gelatin layer in mold. Chill until firm. Yield: 6 to 8 servings.

FAVORITE CHICKEN SALAD

1/2 cup salad dressing or mayonnaise
1 tablespoon lemon juice
1 (5- or 6-ounce) can boned chicken, diced
1 cup thinly sliced celery
2 tablespoons chopped pickles
1 small onion, chopped
Salt and pepper to taste
Lettuce

Combine salad dressing or mayonnaise and lemon juice. Add chicken, celery, pickles, and onion. Season with salt and pepper. Chill. Serve on crisp lettuce. Yield: 4 servings.

CHICKEN SALAD WITH AVOCADO

3 cups cooked, diced chicken
1/2 cup diced celery
1 cup pitted, sliced black olives
1/3 cup mayonnaise
1 1/2 cups diced avocado (1/2-inch pieces)
1 tablespoon lemon juice
Dash cayenne pepper
Lettuce

Blend chicken, celery, and olives with mayonnaise. Cut avocado just before serving and sprinkle lemon juice over it. Fold avocado into the chicken mixture and season to taste, adding cayenne. Serve in lettuce cups and garnish, if desired, with cut pieces of olive or slices of avocado. Yield: 6 servings.

CHICKEN SALAD

1 envelope (1 tablespoon) unflavored gelatin
1/4 cup cold water
1 cup mayonnaise
1/2 pint whipping cream, whipped
1/2 teaspoon salt
2 cups cooked, diced chicken
3/4 cup blanched, toasted, and chopped almonds
3/4 cup seedless green grapes

Soften gelatin in cold water; dissolve over hot water. Cool mixture; then add mayonnaise, whipped cream, and salt. Fold in remaining ingredients and chill. Yield: 8 servings.

JELLIED CHICKEN ALMOND

 1 envelope (1 tablespoon) unflavored
   gelatin
1/4 cup cold water
 1 cup mayonnaise
1/2 pint whipping cream, whipped
1/2 teaspoon salt
1 1/2 cups cooked, diced chicken
3/4 cup chopped blanched almonds,
   toasted
3/4 cup halved green seedless grapes
   Lettuce

Soften gelatin in cold water; dissolve over hot water. Cool slightly; then combine with mayonnaise, whipped cream, and salt. Fold in chicken, almonds, and grapes. Spoon into 6 or 8 individual salad molds. Chill until firm. Unmold on lettuce. Yield: 6 to 8 servings.

Note: For an entirely different flavor, substitute 1 tablespoon chopped pimiento, 1 tablespoon chopped green pepper, and 2 tablespoons chopped onion for the grapes.

CHICKEN AND PINEAPPLE SALAD

 1 envelope (1 tablespoon) unflavored
   gelatin
1 1/2 cups chicken stock, divided
1/2 teaspoon salt
 2 tablespoons lemon juice
1/2 cup crushed pineapple, drained,
   liquid reserved
1 1/2 cups cooked, diced chicken
1/2 cup diced celery
   Salad greens

Sprinkle gelatin on 1/2 cup of chicken stock to soften; place over low heat and stir until gelatin is dissolved. Remove from heat and stir in remaining chicken stock, salt, lemon juice, and 1/4 cup pineapple liquid. Chill to consistency of unbeaten egg white.

Fold in chicken, pineapple, and celery. Turn into a 3-cup mold and chill until firm. Unmold on serving plate and garnish with salad greens. Yield: 4 to 6 servings.

FRUIT-TURKEY SALAD

 1 head lettuce, cored, rinsed, and
   chilled
1/4 cup salad oil
 2 tablespoons vinegar
1/2 to 3/4 teaspoon salt
1/2 teaspoon basil
1/4 teaspoon garlic powder
1/8 teaspoon pepper
 2 cups cooked, cubed turkey or chicken
1/2 onion, thinly sliced into rings
 1 tomato, cubed
1/2 avocado, peeled and sliced
 1 tangerine or orange, peeled and
   sectioned

Reserve 4 whole lettuce leaves for lettuce cups. Shred enough lettuce to make 4 cups; set aside. Blend oil, vinegar, salt, basil, garlic powder, and pepper; combine with turkey or chicken, onion, and tomato; toss gently to mix. Arrange lettuce cups on 4 luncheon plates. Add shredded lettuce; then top with turkey mixture. Garnish with avocado slices and tangerine or orange sections. Serve immediately. Yield: 4 servings.

HOT CRAB SALAD

1/2 cup chopped green pepper
1 small onion, chopped
1/2 cup diced celery
1/4 cup toasted shredded almonds
1 (6 1/2-ounce) can crabmeat
1/2 cup mayonnaise
1/2 teaspoon Worcestershire sauce
1/4 teaspoon salt
Dash pepper
1/2 cup buttered bread crumbs

Combine green pepper, onion, celery, almonds, crabmeat, mayonnaise, and seasonings. Fill individual shells or baking dishes with the mixture and top with bread crumbs. Bake at 350° for 30 minutes and serve hot. Yield: 2 servings.

CRABMEAT SALAD

1 pound crabmeat (preferably backfin lump)
3/4 cup chopped celery
2 tablespoons lemon juice
1 teaspoon salt
1/8 teaspoon pepper
3 tablespoons mayonnaise
1 teaspoon capers

Remove all cartilage from crabmeat. Combine celery, lemon juice, salt, pepper, mayonnaise, and capers. Add crabmeat and mix gently but thoroughly. Keep refrigerated until served. Yield: 4 to 6 servings.

CRAB LOUIS

3/4 cup mayonnaise or salad dressing
1/4 cup chili sauce
2 tablespoons minced parsley
2 teaspoons vinegar
1/2 teaspoon Worcestershire sauce
1/4 teaspoon prepared horseradish
1 pound crabmeat, fresh or canned
Lettuce

Combine first 6 ingredients. Toss lightly with crabmeat. Chill. Serve in lettuce cups. Yield: 4 servings.

DELUXE CRABMEAT SALAD

1 pound crabmeat (preferably backfin lump)
1 (14- or 15-ounce) can artichoke hearts, drained and quartered
1 (8-ounce) can cut green beans, drained
2 hard-cooked eggs, chopped
1/4 cup sliced raw cauliflower
1/2 cup sliced celery
1/4 cup sliced cucumber
1/4 cup sliced green pepper
1 teaspoon salt
1/4 teaspoon pepper
3/4 cup commercial Thousand Island dressing
6 tomato slices
6 lettuce leaves
Radish slices

Remove any remaining shell or cartilage from crabmeat. Combine all ingredients except tomatoes, lettuce, and radishes; toss lightly. Arrange a tomato slice on each lettuce leaf. Place about 1 cup salad on each tomato slice. Garnish with radish slices. Yield: 6 servings.

PEAR AND CRABMEAT SALAD

      2 cups peeled and diced pears
      2 cups crabmeat
      1 cup diced celery
    1/3 cup mayonnaise
      3 tablespoons lemon juice
 1 1/2 teaspoons salt
    1/4 teaspoon pepper
         Lettuce
         Parsley

Combine all ingredients except lettuce and parsley; toss lightly. Chill. Serve on lettuce; garnish with parsley. Yield: 4 servings.

MOLDED SALMON SALAD

      2 envelopes (2 tablespoons) unflavored
         gelatin
    1/2 cup cold water
      1 cup mayonnaise
    1/2 cup half-and-half
      1 tablespoon sugar
    1/2 teaspoon salt
         Juice of 1 lemon
      1 (16-ounce) can salmon, drained and
         flaked
    1/2 cup chopped celery
      2 teaspoons minced onion
         Salad greens
         Pimiento strips

Soften gelatin in cold water; place over hot water until gelatin is dissolved. Combine mayonnaise and half-and-half; stir until smooth. Add sugar, salt, and lemon juice. Stir gelatin into mixture. Add salmon, celery, and onion to mayonnaise mixture. Pour into ring mold; chill until firm. Unmold on salad greens and garnish with pimiento strips. Yield: 6 servings.

CRISPY SALMON SALAD

      1 (16-ounce) can salmon, drained and
         flaked
      4 cups shredded cabbage
    1/4 cup chopped onion
    1/4 cup chopped parsley
      2 hard-cooked eggs, chopped
      1 teaspoon salt
         Dash cayenne pepper
    1/4 teaspoon paprika
      3 tablespoons vinegar
    1/2 cup salad oil
      1 tablespoon chopped pimiento
         (optional)
      1 tablespoon chopped sweet pickle
      1 tablespoon chopped green pepper

Combine salmon, cabbage, onion, parsley, and eggs. Set aside. Combine salt, cayenne, and paprika. Slowly add vinegar and oil, beating thoroughly. Add pimiento, if desired, sweet pickle, and green pepper. Add dressing to salmon mixture and blend thoroughly. Yield: 6 to 8 servings.

SALMON SALAD

      1 (16-ounce) can salmon, drained and
         flaked
    1/2 cup diced celery
    1/2 cup chopped sweet pickle
      2 tablespoons chopped green pepper
    1/2 teaspoon salt
      1 tablespoon lemon juice
    1/3 cup mayonnaise
         Salad greens

Combine all ingredients except salad greens and toss together lightly. Chill thoroughly. Serve on salad greens. This salad also makes an excellent sandwich filling. Yield: 4 servings.

SHRIMP-PEA ASPIC

  2 envelopes (2 tablespoons)
      unflavored gelatin
  3 cups tomato juice, divided
  2 teaspoons cider vinegar
  1 teaspoon sugar
1/2 teaspoon salt
1/2 teaspoon basil
1/2 teaspoon monosodium glutamate
  2 whole cloves
  1 bay leaf, crumbled
1/4 teaspoon hot sauce
  1 cup commercial sour cream
1/2 cup minced celery
1 1/2 cups cooked, peeled, deveined, and
      chopped shrimp
  1 (10-ounce) package frozen peas,
      cooked and drained
      Shrimp and peas for garnish
      (optional)

Soften gelatin in 1/2 cup tomato juice. Combine remaining tomato juice, vinegar, sugar, salt, basil, monosodium glutamate, cloves, and bay leaf; simmer for 5 minutes. Remove cloves and bay leaf. Stir in gelatin and cool; chill until slightly thickened.

Fold in hot sauce, sour cream, celery, shrimp, and peas. Chill in 2-quart mold until salad is firm. Garnish with additional shrimp and peas, if desired. Yield: 6 to 8 servings.

SHRIMP SALAD

  2 (4 1/2- or 5-ounce) cans shrimp,
      drained
  1 cup chopped celery
1/4 cup mayonnaise or salad dressing
  2 tablespoons chopped sweet pickle or
      drained pickle relish
  1 tablespoon grated onion
1/2 teaspoon salt
      Dash pepper
      Salad greens

Cover shrimp with ice water and let stand for 5 minutes; drain. Cut large shrimp in half. Combine all ingredients except salad greens; chill. Serve on salad greens. Yield: 6 servings.

SHRIMP-CUCUMBER SALAD

  1 pound shrimp, cooked, peeled, and
      deveined
1/2 cup thinly sliced celery
1/4 green pepper, thinly sliced
1/2 small cucumber, thinly sliced
1/4 cup commercial Russian dressing
  2 teaspoons lemon juice
1/2 teaspoon salt
      Lettuce cups

Combine shrimp, celery, green pepper, and cucumber. Chill. Just before serving, combine Russian dressing, lemon juice, and salt; add to shrimp mixture and toss. Serve in lettuce cups. Yield: 4 to 6 servings.

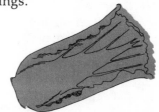

SHRIMP AND APPLE SALAD

  1 cup cooked, peeled, and deveined
      shrimp
  2 medium-size apples, diced
  1 green pepper, cut into narrow strips
  8 stuffed green olives, sliced
1/4 cup mayonnaise
  1 tablespoon lemon or lime juice
      Salad greens

Combine shrimp, apples, green pepper, and olives. Blend mayonnaise with lemon juice. Add to shrimp mixture and toss; chill. Serve on salad greens. Yield: 4 servings.

SHRIMP AND MACARONI SALAD

2 cups cooked macaroni
1/2 teaspoon salt
1/2 cup mayonnaise or salad dressing
2 tablespoons finely chopped sweet pickle
5 hard-cooked eggs, chopped
5 finely chopped ripe olives
1/2 cup finely chopped onion
1/2 cup chopped celery (optional)
2 pounds shrimp, cooked, peeled, and deveined

Combine all ingredients except shrimp. Mix well, place in covered dish and chill. About 30 minutes before serving, stir in shrimp and toss lightly. Yield: 10 to 12 servings.

REFRESHING SHRIMP SALAD

3/4 pound fresh or frozen shrimp (thawed), cooked, peeled, and deveined
1 quart shredded cabbage
1/2 cup sliced green pepper
1 cup commercial sour cream
1 tablespoon lemon juice
1 teaspoon Worcestershire sauce
1/4 teaspoon salt
1/2 teaspoon fresh chopped dill or 1/4 teaspoon dillweed
Dash ground nutmeg
1/2 cup toasted blanched slivered almonds
Salad greens

Cut large shrimp in half. Combine shrimp, cabbage, and green pepper; chill. Combine sour cream, lemon juice, Worcestershire sauce, and seasonings to make dressing; chill. Add almonds and dressing to shrimp mixture; toss lightly. Serve on salad greens. Yield: 6 servings.

TOMATO-SHRIMP SALAD

2 cups tomato juice
1 tablespoon vinegar
Salt and pepper to taste
1 (3-ounce) package lemon-flavored gelatin
1 (5-ounce) can shrimp, drained and chopped
1 cup sliced stuffed olives
2 cups diced celery
1 hard-cooked egg, chopped
Mayonnaise or commercial blue cheese dressing

Combine tomato juice, vinegar, salt, and pepper and bring to a boil. Remove from heat and pour over gelatin. Stir to dissolve; let cool.
After gelatin has cooled, stir in shrimp, olives, celery, and egg. Pour into a 1 1/2-quart mold and chill until firm. Serve with mayonnaise or blue cheese dressing. Yield: 6 servings.

SHRIMP-AVOCADO SALAD

1/2 head lettuce, washed, drained, and torn into bite-size pieces
1 cup grapefruit sections, drained
1 cup cooked, peeled, and deveined shrimp
1/4 cup onion rings
1 avocado
2 tablespoons lemon juice
3 tablespoons salad oil
1/2 teaspoon salt
1/4 teaspoon pepper

In salad bowl combine lettuce, grapefruit, shrimp, and onion. Arrange over salad leaves. Slice avocado; dip into lemon juice to prevent discoloration. Add to salad. Mix remaining lemon juice with salad oil, salt, and pepper. Beat vigorously with beater. Pour over salad just before serving. Toss lightly. Yield: 6 servings.

SHRIMP-VEGETABLE ASPIC

2 (3-ounce) packages lemon-flavored gelatin
1 1/2 cups boiling water
1/2 cup chili sauce
2 cups tomato juice
1 tablespoon sweet pickle relish
5 large stuffed olives, sliced
2 green onions, chopped
1 cup chopped celery
1 pound shrimp, cooked, peeled, and deveined
Shredded lettuce
1 cup mayonnaise
2 tablespoons chili sauce
1 tablespoon prepared horseradish

Dissolve gelatin in boiling water; add 1/2 cup chili sauce and tomato juice. Chill until consistency of unbeaten egg white. Add pickle relish, olives, onions, celery, and shrimp. Pour salad mixture into oiled 8-cup ring mold. Chill overnight. Turn out onto round platter lined with shredded lettuce. Combine mayonnaise, 2 tablespoons chili sauce, and horseradish; serve as dressing. Yield: 8 servings.

TUNA-TATER SALAD

2 (6 1/2- or 7-ounce) cans tuna fish, drained and broken into chunks
2 cups cooked, chopped potatoes
3 hard-cooked eggs, chopped
1/2 cup grated carrot
2/3 cup salad dressing or mayonnaise
2 tablespoons chopped onion
1 teaspoon salt
Pepper to taste
Salad greens

Combine all ingredients except salad greens; cover and chill. Serve on salad greens. Yield: 6 servings.

HAWAIIAN TUNA PARTY SALAD

1/2 cup mayonnaise
1/4 cup chutney
2 teaspoons curry powder
1/2 teaspoon salt
1 cup chopped celery
1 (20-ounce) can pineapple tidbits, drained
3 (7-ounce) cans tuna fish, drained and flaked
2 cups cooked rice
Slivered almonds
Lettuce

Mix mayonnaise, chutney, curry, and salt. Combine celery, pineapple, tuna fish, and rice.
Combine the two mixtures and garnish with slivered almonds. Serve in lettuce cups. Yield: 8 servings.

PATIO SPECIAL TUNA SALAD

2 (7-ounce) cans tuna fish, drained and flaked
1/2 cup chopped celery
1/4 cup pickle relish, drained
1/2 teaspoon lemon juice
1 teaspoon finely chopped onion
1/3 cup mayonnaise
Sliced cucumbers
Tomatoes, sliced 1/2 inch thick

Combine tuna fish, celery, relish, lemon juice, onion, and mayonnaise. Mix well. To serve, place a cucumber slice on a tomato slice and top with a scoop of tuna salad. Yield: 4 to 6 servings.

FESTIVE TUNA-RICE SALAD

   3 cups cooked long grain rice, cooled
   1 (7-ounce) can light tuna fish,
     drained and flaked
   3 hard-cooked eggs, chopped
   2 tablespoons sweet pickle relish
1 1/2 teaspoons minced, fresh or frozen,
     chives
   1/2 cup chopped celery
   1 large pimiento, drained and
     chopped
   1/2 cup mayonnaise
   1 teaspoon prepared mustard
   1/2 teaspoon lemon juice
     Dash salt and pepper
     Paprika

Combine rice, tuna fish, eggs, relish, chives, celery, and pimiento. In another bowl mix mayonnaise, mustard, lemon juice, salt, and pepper. Pour over rice mixture and toss. Chill thoroughly. Serve in a salad bowl and sprinkle with paprika. Yield: 8 servings.

MOLDED TUNA SALAD

   2 (2/3 envelope) teaspoons unflavored
     gelatin
   2/3 cup cold water
   1 (7-ounce) can tuna fish, drained and
     flaked
   3/4 cup chopped celery
   2 tablespoons finely chopped onion
   1/2 teaspoon salt
   3 tablespoons sweet pickle relish
   1/3 cup mayonnaise or salad dressing
     Lettuce

Soften gelatin in cold water; heat over boiling water to dissolve. Cool. Combine tuna fish, celery, onion, salt, pickle relish, and mayonnaise or salad dressing. Add to cool gelatin and stir well. Chill until firm. Unmold and serve on lettuce. Yield: 4 servings.

FRESH SNAP BEAN AND
TUNA FISH SALAD

   1 pound (3 1/2 cups, cut) young, tender,
     fresh snap beans
   1 teaspoon salt
     Boiling water
   1/4 cup olive or salad oil
   2 teaspoons lemon juice
   1/8 teaspoon freshly ground black
     pepper
   1 (7-ounce) can tuna fish, drained and
     broken into chunks

Wash beans, remove tips, and cut into 1 1/2-inch lengths. Place in a saucepan with 1 teaspoon salt and 1/2 inch boiling water. Bring to boiling point and cook uncovered for 5 minutes. Cover and continue cooking until beans are crisp-tender, about 10 minutes. Combine oil, lemon juice, and black pepper; mix well. Drain beans and while hot add the oil mixture. Mix lightly. Turn into a serving dish. Scatter tuna fish chunks over top. Serve hot or cold as a main-dish salad. Yield: 4 servings.

Cheese, Egg, Rice, and Pasta Salads

Combine mayonnaise or salad dressing, mustard, and garlic salt; add eggs, celery, parsley, and pimiento; mix lightly and press into four 6-ounce custard cups; chill 2 hours. Unmold on lettuce leaves. Garnish with tomato wedges and cucumber slices. Yield: 4 servings.

CHEESE AND BACON SALAD

- 3 slices bacon, fried and crumbled, drippings reserved
- 2 tablespoons lemon juice
- 1/2 head lettuce, torn into bite-size pieces
- 1 cup shredded Cheddar cheese
  Salt to taste

To bacon and drippings, add lemon juice. Toss lettuce and cheese together; sprinkle with salt. Top with hot bacon mixture and toss well. Serve immediately. Yield: 4 servings.

CALICO RICE SALAD

- 3 cups cooked rice
- 6 hard-cooked eggs, chopped
- 1/2 cup chopped onion
- 1/4 cup chopped pimiento
- 1/4 cup chopped green pepper
- 1/4 cup chopped celery
- 1/4 cup chopped dill pickle
- 1 teaspoon salt
  Dash pepper
- 1/4 cup commercial French dressing
- 1/3 cup mayonnaise or salad dressing
- 2 tablespoons prepared mustard
  Lettuce

Combine first 9 ingredients. Combine French dressing, mayonnaise, and mustard; add to rice mixture and toss to coat ingredients. Chill well. Serve on lettuce. Yield: 5 to 6 servings.

MARDI GRAS EGG SALAD

- 1/2 cup mayonnaise or salad dressing
- 4 teaspoons prepared mustard
- 1/2 teaspoon garlic salt
- 8 hard-cooked eggs, chopped
- 1/2 cup chopped celery
- 2 tablespoons chopped parsley
- 1 tablespoon chopped pimiento
  Lettuce
- 2 tomatoes cut into wedges
  Cucumber slices

TWO-CHEESE LUNCHEON SALAD

     1 cup uncooked macaroni
   1/2 cup thinly sliced celery
     2 large apples, cubed
   1/4 teaspoon salt
   1/2 pound Swiss cheese, cut into 1/4-inch
        cubes
     1 cup commercial sour cream
     1 tablespoon lemon juice
     1 tablespoon honey
        Lettuce cups
     1 cup shredded Cheddar cheese

Cook macaroni according to package directions; drain, rinse, and chill. Combine macaroni, celery, apples, salt, and Swiss cheese; set aside. Combine sour cream, lemon juice, and honey; combine with macaroni mixture. Serve in lettuce cups; sprinkle with Cheddar cheese. Yield: 6 servings.

SHELL MACARONI SALAD

     1 (8-ounce) package elbow or shell
        macaroni
        Commercial French dressing
 1 1/2 cups chopped celery
     1 tablespoon minced sweet onion
   1/4 cup chopped tart cucumber pickle
        or stuffed olives
   1/4 cup minced green pepper
     1 cup finely cubed cheese, ham,
        cooked meat, or fish
   3/4 cup mayonnaise or desired salad
        dressing
        Salt to taste

Cook macaroni according to package directions; drain thoroughly and rinse with cold water. Add enough French dressing to coat the macaroni; chill thoroughly. Drain off any excess dressing and combine macaroni with other ingredients, using enough mayonnaise or salad dressing to bind the ingredients together. Yield: 6 servings.

ORIENTAL EGG SALAD

   3/4 cup uncooked regular rice
   1/2 medium-size onion, finely chopped
   3/4 pound cooked shrimp, shelled and
        deveined
     2 cucumbers, chopped
     5 hard-cooked eggs, divided
 1 1/4 cups commercial French dressing,
        divided
        Lettuce
 1 1/4 tablespoons capers
 2 1/2 tablespoons catsup

Cook rice according to package directions. Drain and combine with onion, shrimp, cucumber, 3 eggs which have been chopped, and 1/2 cup French dressing. Chill mixture in refrigerator. Spread lettuce leaves in salad bowl; put rice mixture on top. Grate remaining eggs, and sprinkle around edge and in center of salad bowl. Mix remaining French dressing with capers and catsup, and pour over salad. Yield: 6 servings.

EGG AND BAKED BEAN SALAD

     6 hard-cooked eggs, chopped and
        chilled
     1 (20-ounce) can pork and beans,
        drained and chilled
   1/2 cup minced onion
     1 tablespoon chili sauce
     1 tablespoon mayonnaise
     1 teaspoon dry mustard
   1/4 teaspoon salt
        Dash pepper
        Salad greens
     3 slices bacon, fried and crumbled
     3 tablespoons minced parsley

Mix eggs, beans, and onion. Combine chili sauce, mayonnaise, mustard, salt, and pepper. Add to egg mixture. Place in chilled salad bowl lined with salad greens.

Just before serving, sprinkle bacon and parsley over top. Yield: 6 servings.

RICE AND VEGETABLE SALAD BOWL

1/4 cup water
1/4 cup commercial Italian dressing
1/2 cup uncooked instant rice
1/2 (10-ounce) package frozen peas, cooked and drained
  2 tablespoons chopped green onion with tops
1/4 cup cooked sliced mushrooms, drained
1/4 cup diced cucumber
  2 tablespoons sliced stuffed olives
1/3 cup mayonnaise or salad dressing
     Lettuce
  1 tomato, cut into wedges

Combine water and Italian dressing in saucepan; bring to boil. Remove from heat. Add rice; cover, and let stand 5 minutes. Fluff rice with fork. Add peas and mix well. Chill.

Add onion, mushrooms, cucumber, olives, and mayonnaise; mix well. Refrigerate until serving time. Serve on lettuce; garnish with tomato. Yield: 4 servings.

PASTA SALAD

  1 (5-ounce) package vermicelli
  5 hard-cooked eggs, chopped
1 1/2 cups finely chopped celery
  1 cup finely chopped sweet pickle
  2 to 2 1/2 teaspoons onion salt
  1 cup mayonnaise
     Lettuce leaves
  1 (7 1/2-ounce) can crabmeat, drained and flaked
     Paprika

Break vermicelli into pieces and cook according to package directions. Drain and rinse; let cool. Add eggs, celery, pickle, onion salt, and mayonnaise to vermicelli. Mix lightly and chill. To serve, mound vermicelli mixture on bed of lettuce leaves. Top with crabmeat and sprinkle with paprika. Yield: 6 to 8 servings.

MACARONI TWISTS SALAD

1 1/2 cups uncooked macaroni twists
  1 small onion, finely grated
  1 hard-cooked egg, chopped
  1 tomato, diced
1/4 cup chopped pickle
  1 cup shredded lettuce
  2 tablespoons mayonnaise
  1 teaspoon prepared mustard
     Dash paprika
     Salt and pepper to taste
  4 slices bacon, fried, crumbled, and divided

Cook macaroni according to package directions; drain and cool. Combine onion, egg, tomato, pickle, lettuce, mayonnaise, mustard, paprika, salt, pepper, and half the crumbled bacon; add to macaroni and toss lightly. Sprinkle remaining bacon on top. Yield: about 6 servings.

Salad Dressings

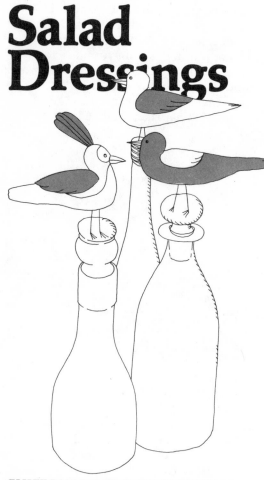

CHIFFONADE FRENCH DRESSING

- 1 1/2 teaspoons salt
- 1/4 teaspoon pepper
- 1/4 teaspoon dry mustard
- 1 cup salad oil
- 1/3 cup vinegar
- 1 hard-cooked egg, chopped
- 1 teaspoon grated onion
- 2 tablespoons chopped green pepper
- 1 tablespoon chopped celery
- 1 tablespoon chopped parsley

Combine salt, pepper, and mustard. Stir in oil and vinegar. Add remaining ingredients. Pour into jar and shake well. Yield: 1 pint.

CREAMY BLUE CHEESE DRESSING

- 1/2 cup commercial sour cream
- 2 tablespoons mayonnaise
  Juice of 1/2 lemon
  Tops of 2 green onions, chopped
- 3/4 cup (about 4 ounces) crumbled blue cheese
- 1/2 teaspoon Worcestershire sauce
  Salt (optional)
  Sugar (optional)

Combine all ingredients and mix well. Add a pinch salt and a little sugar, if desired. Yield: 1 1/4 cups.

SOUR CREAM-FRUIT SALAD DRESSING

- 1 teaspoon grated orange rind
- 2 tablespoons orange juice
- 2 tablespoons lemon juice
- 1 tablespoon honey
- 1/2 teaspoon dry mustard
- 1 teaspoon salt
- 1/4 teaspoon paprika
- 1 cup commercial sour cream

Blend all ingredients except sour cream. Fold mixture into sour cream. Chill thoroughly before serving. Serve with fruit salads. Yield: about 1 1/4 cups.

GREEN GODDESS SALAD DRESSING

- 1 cup mayonnaise
- 1/2 cup commercial sour cream
- 1/4 teaspoon garlic powder
- 2 green onions with tops, chopped
- 2 tablespoons lemon juice
- 1/4 cup chopped parsley
- 1/4 teaspoon pepper
- 1/4 cup chopped green pepper
- 3 anchovy filets
  Dash Worcestershire sauce

Place all ingredients in blender. Cover and blend 10 seconds on high speed or until pale green and smooth. Yield: about 2 cups.

CRANBERRY-WHIPPED CREAM DRESSING

1/4 pint whipping cream, whipped
1/2 cup mayonnaise
1/3 cup strained cranberry sauce

Combine whipped cream and mayonnaise. Fold in cranberry sauce. Serve over turkey or chicken salad. Yield: 1 1/2 cups.

TOMATO SALAD DRESSING

1 (10 3/4-ounce) can tomato soup, undiluted
3/4 cup vinegar
1/2 cup salad oil
1/4 cup sugar
1 tablespoon Worcestershire sauce
3 tablespoons grated onion
1 teaspoon salt
1 tablespoon dry mustard
1 teaspoon paprika
2 cloves garlic

Combine all ingredients except garlic in a quart jar; shake well. Add garlic and let stand for garlic flavor to develop. Chill. Remove garlic before serving. Yield: 1 quart.

LOW-CALORIE FRENCH DRESSING

3 tablespoons salad oil
3/4 teaspoon salt
1 teaspoon sugar
1/8 teaspoon paprika
1/2 teaspoon dry mustard
1/4 teaspoon hot sauce
1 cup grapefruit juice, divided
2 teaspoons cornstarch

Combine salad oil, salt, sugar, paprika, dry mustard, and hot sauce in small mixing bowl. Blend together 1/2 cup grapefruit juice and 2 teaspoons cornstarch in small saucepan; cook over low heat, stirring constantly, until mixture thickens and comes to a boil. Add to salad oil mixture; beat with rotary beater until smooth. Beat in remaining 1/2 cup grapefruit juice. Yield: 1 cup.

Note: About 35 calories per tablespoon.

ORANGE-FRENCH DRESSING

1 (6-ounce) can frozen orange juice concentrate, undiluted
3/4 cup salad oil
1/4 cup vinegar
3 tablespoons sugar
1/2 teaspoon dry mustard
1/4 teaspoon salt
1/4 teaspoon hot sauce

Combine all ingredients. Chill. Yield: 1 3/4 cups.

WATERCRESS MAYONNAISE

1 1/2 cups mayonnaise
   1 bunch (about 2 cups) watercress, chopped
   1 medium-size clove garlic, minced
1/4 cup milk

Place all ingredients in blender; blend until watercress is finely chopped. Serve as a salad dressing or as a sauce for cold meat. Yield: 2 cups.

TOURNAY'S GREEN SALAD DRESSING

   1 bunch (5 or 6) green onions
3/4 cup vinegar
   2 teaspoons garlic salt
   2 tablespoons sugar
1/4 to 1/2 teaspoon freshly ground black pepper
   2 cups salad oil
    Juice of 1 lemon

Put onions (tops and all) into blender and blend until well chopped. Add vinegar, garlic salt, sugar, and pepper. Add salad oil slowly. Stir in lemon juice. Yield: about 3 cups.

CUCUMBER-MAYONNAISE DRESSING

1/2 cup mayonnaise
1/4 cup chopped cucumber
   1 tablespoon chopped parsley

Combine all ingredients; serve with tomato aspic. Yield: 3/4 cup.

SALAD DRESSING FOR SLAW

1/3 cup finely chopped onion
1/3 cup commercial French dressing
1/4 cup sugar
    Mayonnaise (optional)

Combine first 3 ingredients and let sit in refrigerator. Dressing will be better if allowed to sit for 3 days before using. To make a creamier dressing, 3 tablespoons mayonnaise may be added, if desired, just before serving. Yield: about 3/4 cup.

TOMATO DRESSING

   1 cup salad oil
1/3 cup vinegar
   1 (8-ounce) can tomato sauce
   2 tablespoons lemon juice
   1 small onion, grated
   1 clove garlic, minced or crushed
   3 tablespoons sugar
1/4 teaspoon pepper
   1 teaspoon salt
    Lettuce wedges

Combine all ingredients except lettuce; shake or beat to blend thoroughly. Chill several hours to blend flavors. Beat well before using. Serve over lettuce wedges. Yield: about 2 1/2 cups.

WILTED LETTUCE DRESSING

   2 tablespoons bacon drippings
1/2 teaspoon salt
1/4 teaspoon dry mustard
   1 teaspoon sugar
   1 tablespoon vinegar
    Lettuce

Mix all ingredients except lettuce in saucepan and heat to sizzling. Pour over leaf lettuce. Yield: 1/4 cup.

RIVERSIDE DRESSING

1 (10 3/4-ounce) can tomato soup,
   undiluted
1/2 cup salad oil
1/2 cup vinegar
1/2 cup sugar
1 teaspoon Worcestershire sauce
1 teaspoon dry mustard
1 teaspoon salt
1 medium-size onion, grated
1 clove garlic, split

Combine all ingredients except garlic and beat together. Add garlic and store in a glass jar. Keep in refrigerator. Remove garlic and shake well before serving. Yield: 2 1/2 cups.

COOKED SALAD DRESSING

2 teaspoons dry mustard
1 teaspoon salt
   Dash paprika
2 tablespoons sugar
1/2 envelope (1 1/2 teaspoons)
   unflavored gelatin
4 teaspoons cold water
3/4 cup hot water
1 tablespoon melted butter or
   margarine
1 egg, well beaten
1/4 cup cider vinegar

Mix seasonings. Soften gelatin in cold water. Add hot water to mustard mixture; stir until blended. To this add gelatin and butter or margarine; stir until gelatin dissolves. Stir hot mixture slowly into

beaten egg. Cook, stirring constantly, until mixture begins to thicken. Remove from heat; stir in vinegar. Pour into jar; set aside to cool and thicken. Yield: 1 1/4 cups.

SPECIAL FRUIT SALAD DRESSING

1/2 cup sugar
1 teaspoon salt
3 tablespoons all-purpose flour
2 eggs, slightly beaten
1/4 cup vinegar
1 1/2 cups pineapple juice

Combine dry ingredients in saucepan; add eggs and mix well. Add vinegar and pineapple juice. Cook over low heat until thick and smooth, stirring constantly. Chill thoroughly. Serve on molded, frozen, or fresh fruit salad. Yield: 2 cups.

BEER DRESSING

3/4 cup salad oil
1/2 cup beer
1 1/2 teaspoons Worcestershire sauce
1 (10 3/4-ounce) can tomato soup,
   undiluted
1/2 small onion, minced
1/2 clove garlic, crushed
1 1/2 teaspoons sugar
1 teaspoon salt
1 1/2 teaspoons prepared horseradish

Put all ingredients into blender and blend until smooth. Chill until ready to serve. (It may be necessary to whirl in blender again before serving.) Yield: 3 1/2 cups.

75

FAVORITE POPPY-SEED DRESSING

1 teaspoon salt
1 teaspoon dry mustard
1 teaspoon paprika
1 teaspoon poppy seeds
1/2 cup light corn syrup
1/4 to 1/3 cup vinegar
1 cup corn oil

Combine all ingredients in a small bowl; beat until well blended and thickened. Place in a covered container and chill several hours. Shake before serving. Yield: 1 3/4 cups.

POPPY-SEED DRESSING

1/4 cup sugar
1/2 cup white vinegar
1 teaspoon dry mustard
1 teaspoon salt
1 clove garlic, crushed
1 cup salad oil
1/3 large onion, grated
4 teaspoons poppy seeds

Combine all ingredients in pint jar. Mix well and let sit at least 6 hours before serving. Yield: 1 1/4 cups.

TARRAGON DRESSING

6 tablespoons salad oil
3 tablespoons tarragon vinegar
1 1/2 teaspoons dry white wine
1/2 teaspoon salt
1/4 teaspoon freshly ground black pepper
1 1/2 teaspoons paprika
1/2 teaspoon sugar
Generous pinch dried tarragon
1/2 teaspoon grated onion

Put all ingredients into jar and shake well. Prepare dressing the day before you plan to use it. Yield: about 2/3 cup.

ANCHOVY SALAD DRESSING

1 (2-ounce) can anchovies, mashed (include half the oil)
1 bunch green onions and 1 inch of tops, chopped
1 tablespoon Worcestershire sauce Pepper to taste
1/2 to 2/3 cup commercial Italian dressing
1/3 cup salad oil
1/3 cup tarragon or wine vinegar

Combine all ingredients and shake vigorously. Excellent on any tossed green salad; keeps well. Yield: about 1 1/2 cups.

SAVORY SALAD DRESSING

1/4 teaspoon chili powder
1/8 teaspoon paprika
Dash cayenne pepper
1/8 teaspoon freshly ground black pepper
1/4 teaspoon garlic powder
1/2 teaspoon dry mustard
1/2 teaspoon salt
1 teaspoon grated onion
2/3 cup salad oil
1/3 cup cider vinegar

Combine dry ingredients in small bowl of electric mixer. Add onion, then gradually beat in oil. When well blended, add vinegar and beat again. Best if made several days before using. Yield: about 1 1/4 cups.

Alternate method: Place all ingredients in jar with tight-fitting cover; shake vigorously until blended.

SOUR CREAM-ROQUEFORT DRESSING

1 cup commercial sour cream
2 green onions, finely minced
2 tablespoons mayonnaise
2 to 3 tablespoons lemon juice
2/3 cup crumbled Roquefort cheese
Salt and pepper to taste

Stir all ingredients together by hand, blending thoroughly. Chill several hours before serving. Yield: 8 to 10 servings.

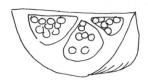

WINE FRENCH DRESSING

1 teaspoon sugar
1 teaspoon salt
1/2 teaspoon dry mustard
1 teaspoon Worcestershire sauce
1/3 cup catsup
1/4 cup dry red wine
1 teaspoon scraped onion
1/4 cup wine vinegar
3/4 cup salad oil

Combine all ingredients in jar with tight-fitting cover. Shake until thoroughly blended; chill. Best if made the day before using. Yield: about 1 1/2 cups.

MAYONNAISE HARVEY

1 egg
1 1/2 cups salad oil
1 1/2 tablespoons lemon juice
1/4 cup grated Parmesan cheese
1/2 teaspoon commercial steak sauce
1/2 teaspoon Worcestershire sauce
1 clove garlic, crushed
3 drops hot sauce
Salt and pepper to taste

Beat egg thoroughly in small bowl of electric mixer. Add oil a teaspoon at a time until half has been added; beat in lemon juice, then remaining oil in several portions. Blend in all other ingredients and chill before serving. Yield: about 1 1/2 cups.

ITALIAN DRESSING

1/3 cup tarragon vinegar
1 teaspoon salt
1 teaspoon dry mustard
1 teaspoon paprika
1/4 teaspoon freshly ground black pepper
2/3 cup salad or olive oil
1 clove garlic, slashed
2 teaspoons drained capers
1/2 teaspoon oregano
1/2 teaspoon minced parsley

Combine vinegar, salt, dry mustard, paprika, and pepper in a jar with tight cover. Shake until salt is dissolved. Add oil, shake again; add garlic, capers, oregano, and parsley. Give the jar a final shake, then let dressing stand until needed. Before using, remove garlic and shake the jar again. Yield: about 1 cup.

THOUSAND ISLAND DRESSING

1 cup mayonnaise
1/2 cup chili sauce
1 (2-ounce) bottle stuffed olives, diced
1/2 cup shredded Cheddar cheese
2 hard-cooked eggs, diced
Juice of 1/2 lemon

Blend all ingredients. Allow dressing to sit for awhile so that flavors may blend. Yield: about 2 1/2 cups.

SHERRY FRENCH DRESSING

  1 small clove garlic
  2 small white onions, finely chopped
  1 teaspoon sugar
  1 teaspoon salt
1/3 cup wine vinegar
  1 to 2 tablespoons dry sherry
1/4 teaspoon freshly ground black
     pepper
3/4 cup olive or salad oil
     Juice of 1/2 lemon

With mortar and pestle or wooden spoon mash garlic, onion, sugar, and salt, blending until pastelike. Add vinegar, sherry, and pepper. Beat in 2 tablespoonfuls oil at a time; then beat in lemon juice. Taste to check seasonings and pour over salad. Yield: 6 servings.

OLIVE DRESSING

1/2 cup salad oil
  3 tablespoons cider vinegar
  1 teaspoon salt
1/8 teaspoon white pepper
1/4 teaspoon paprika
  1 tablespoon minced fresh parsley
  1 tablespoon minced chives
  3 tablespoons minced stuffed olives

Place all ingredients in a jar with tight-fitting cover and shake vigorously until dressing is blended. Cover and store in refrigerator until ready to use; shake again before pouring over salad. Yield: 3/4 cup.

AVOCADO DRESSING

  1 egg, slightly beaten
1/2 teaspoon dry mustard
1/2 cup salad oil
1/4 teaspoon hot sauce
     Juice of 2 large lemons
  1 teaspoon Worcestershire sauce
1/2 teaspoon salt
1/2 teaspoon white pepper
  2 medium-size avocados, peeled,
     stones removed
  3 fresh shallots (use tops only)
  1 clove garlic, peeled and freshly
     ground, or garlic powder to taste
  1 ounce anchovy filets
1/2 cup mayonnaise
1/2 teaspoon saffron

Combine egg and mustard; add oil and mix thoroughly. Add hot sauce, lemon juice, Worcestershire, salt, and pepper. Mix well.

Grind avocados, garlic, and anchovies into a smooth paste. Blend gently but thoroughly with other ingredients. Add mayonnaise and saffron and mix thoroughly. Pour into container and chill for 2 hours. Serve as a dressing for green salad. Yield: 1 1/2 pints.

POPPY-SEED DRESSING
FOR FRUIT SALAD

1/3 cup honey
  1 teaspoon salt
  2 tablespoons vinegar
  1 tablespoon prepared mustard
3/4 cup salad oil
  2 to 3 teaspoons poppy seeds

Combine honey, salt, vinegar, and mustard; gradually add salad oil, beating thoroughly until mixture is well blended. Stir in poppy seeds. Cover and chill several hours before serving. Shake well before serving. Yield: about 1 1/4 cups.

Index

Index